Sample Papers for Exam Success

Computer Science

for Class XII

(As per the CBSE Syllabus Code 083)

Sangita Chadha

www.bpbonline.com

FIRST EDITION 2021

ISBN: 978-93-90684-24-3

Distributors:

BPB PUBLICATIONS
20, Ansari Road, Darya Ganj
New Delhi-110002
Ph: 23254990/23254991

DECCAN AGENCIES
4-3-329, Bank Street,
Hyderabad-500195
Ph: 24756967/24756400

MICRO MEDIA
Shop No. 5, Mahendra Chambers,
150 DN Rd. Next to Capital Cinema,
V.T. (C.S.T.) Station, MUMBAI-400 001
Ph: 22078296/22078297

BPB BOOK CENTRE
376 Old Lajpat Rai Market,
Delhi-110006
Ph: 23861747

To View Complete BPB Publications Catalogue Scan the QR Code:

Published by Manish Jain for BPB Publications, 20 Ansari Road, Darya Ganj, New Delhi-110002 and Printed by him at Repro India Ltd, Mumbai

www.bpbonline.com

About the Author

Sangita Chadha has been working as Head of Computer Department in Ambience Public School, Safdarjung Enclave, New Delhi from last 12 years. She has over twenty years of experience in the field of education; teaching Computer Science, Informatics Practices and Multimedia & Web Technology to grades XI and XII; and has been multifold responsibilities at her school (Result In-charge, ERP, Website, Almanac, Magazine). She is a passionate learner and committed educator consistently working to make learning enjoyable for the learners. Her foremost classroom pedagogy is centered around project-based learning. She has conducted ICT and Net safety workshops for all stakeholders. She has been part of the curriculum development team for classes IX and X Information and Communication Technology, NCERT. She has co-authored class IX and X ICT for NCERT. She also co-authored Class XII Informatics Practices and Computer Science, NCERT. She has conducted Teacher Training workshops for SCERT Teachers.

Preface

With the recent revision of the syllabus for Computer Science, the CBSE has changed the marking scheme and the exam pattern. All this has been kept in mind while writing this sample paper.

The book in your hand is strictly based on the new CBSE syllabus and promises to deliver the content keeping in mind the learning objectives of the computer science subject.

The papers are divided into two Parts - A and B. Each part is compulsory.

Part - A has 2 sections.

(a) Section-I consists of short questions, to be answered in one word or one line.

(b) Section-II consist of two case studies questions. Each case study has 4 case-based subparts. An examinee has to attempt any 4 out of the 5 subparts.

Part - B is Descriptive Paper and has three sections.

(a) Section-I consists of short questions of 2 marks each in which two questions have internal options.

(b) Section-II consists of long questions of 3 marks each in which two questions have internal options.

(c) Section-III consists of very long questions of 5 marks each in which one question has an internal option.

Note: All programming questions are to be answered using Python Language only.

Downloading the coloured images:

Please follow the link to download the *Coloured Images* of the book:

https://rebrand.ly/a7fd2

Errata

We take immense pride in our work at BPB Publications and follow best practices to ensure the accuracy of our content to provide with an indulging reading experience to our subscribers. Our readers are our mirrors, and we use their inputs to reflect and improve upon human errors, if any, that may have occurred during the publishing processes involved. To let us maintain the quality and help us reach out to any readers who might be having difficulties due to any unforeseen errors, please write to us at:

errata@bpbonline.com

Your support, suggestions and feedbacks are highly appreciated by the BPB Publications' Family.

BPB is searching for authors like you

If you're interested in becoming an author for BPB, please visit **www.bpbonline.com** and apply today. We have worked with thousands of developers and tech professionals, just like you, to help them share their insight with the global tech community. You can make a general application, apply for a specific hot topic that we are recruiting an author for, or submit your own idea.

The code bundle for the book is also hosted on GitHub at **https://github.com/bpbpublications/Sample-paper-for-exam-success**. In case there's an update to the code, it will be updated on the existing GitHub repository.

We also have other code bundles from our rich catalog of books and videos available at **https://github.com/bpbpublications**. Check them out!

PIRACY

If you come across any illegal copies of our works in any form on the internet, we would be grateful if you would provide us with the location address or website name. Please contact us at **business@bpbonline.com** with a link to the material.

If you are interested in becoming an author

If there is a topic that you have expertise in, and you are interested in either writing or contributing to a book, please visit **www.bpbonline.com**.

REVIEWS

Please leave a review. Once you have read and used this book, why not leave a review on the site that you purchased it from? Potential readers can then see and use your unbiased opinion to make purchase decisions, we at BPB can understand what you think about our products, and our authors can see your feedback on their book. Thank you!

For more information about BPB, please visit **www.bpbonline.com**.

Table of Contents

CBSE
Sample Paper
2020-21

Computer Science (083)

CBSE Sample Question Paper 2020-21

M.M.: 70 **Time: 3 hrs**

General Instructions

1. This question paper contains two parts A and B. Each part is compulsory.
2. Both Part A and Part B have choices.
3. Part-A has 2 sections:
   a. Section – I is short answer questions, to be answered in one word or one line.
   b. Section – II has two case studies questions. Each case study has 4 case-based subparts. An examinee is to attempt any 4 out of the 5 subparts.
4. Part - B is Descriptive Paper.
5. Part- B has three sections
   a. Section-I is short answer questions of 2 marks each in which two question have internal options.
   b. Section-II is long answer questions of 3 marks each in which two questions have internal options.
   c. Section-III is very long answer questions of 5 marks each in which one question has internal option.
6. All programming questions are to be answered using Python Language only.

PART – A

SECTION – I

Attempt any 15 questions from question numbers 1 to 21. Each question carries 1 mark. **(1 × 15 = 15 marks)**

1. Find the invalid identifier from the following: 1

(a) MyName (b) True (c) 2ndName (d) My_Name

2. Given the lists L=[1,3,6,82,5,7,11,92] , write the output of print(L[2:5]) 1

3. Write the full form of CSV. 1

4. Identify the valid arithmetic operator in Python from the following: 1

(a) ? (b) < (c) ** (d) and

5. Suppose a tuple T is declared as T = (10, 12, 43, 39), which of the following is incorrect? 1

(a) print(T[1]) (b) T[2] = -29 (c) print(max(T)) (d) print(len(T))

6. Write a statement in Python to declare a dictionary whose keys are 1, 2, 3 and values are Monday, Tuesday and Wednesday respectively. 1

7. A tuple is declared as

T = (2,5,6,9,8)

What will be the value of sum(T)? 1

8. Name the built-in mathematical function / method that is used to return an absolute value of a number. 1

9. Name the protocol that is used to send emails. 1

10. Your friend Ranjana complaints that somebody has created a fake profile on Facebook and defaming her character with abusive comments and pictures. Identify the type of cybercrime for these situations. 1

11. In SQL, name the clause that is used to display the tuples in ascending order of an attribute. 1

12. In SQL, what is the use of IS NULL operator? 1

13. Write any one aggregate function used in SQL. 1

14. Which of the following is a DDL command? 1

(a) SELECT (b) ALTER (c) INSERT (d) UPDATE

15. Name the transmission media best suitable for connecting to hilly areas. 1

16. Identify the valid declaration of L: 1

L = ['Mon', '23', 'hello', '60.5']

(a) dictionary (b) string (c) tuple (d) list

17. If the following code is executed, what will be the output of the following code?

name="ComputerSciencewithPython"

print(name[3:10]) 1

18. In SQL, write the query to display the list of tables stored in a database. 1

19. Write the expanded form of Wi-Fi. 1

20. Which of the following types of table constraints will prevent the entry of duplicate rows? 1

(a) Unique (b) Distinct (c) Primary Key (d) NULL

21. Rearrange the following terms in increasing order of data transfer rates. 1

Gbps, Mbps, Tbps, Kbps, bps

SECTION – II

Consists of case study questions and are compulsory to attempt. Attempt any 4 sub parts from each question. Each sub part carries 1 mark. (4 + 4 = 8 marks)

22. A departmental store MyStore is considering to maintain their inventory using SQL to store the data. As a database administer, Abhay has decided that:

- Name of the database - mystore
- Name of the table - STORE
- The attributes of STORE are as follows:

  ItemNo: numeric

  ItemName: character of size 20

  Scode: numeric

  Quantity: numeric

Table: STORE

ItemNo	ItemName	Scode	Quantity
2005	Sharpener Classic	23	60
2003	Ball Pen 0.25	22	50
2002	Get Pen Premium	21	150
2006	Get Pen Classic	21	250
2001	Eraser Small	22	220
2004	Eraser Big	22	110
2009	Ball Pen 0.5	21	180

(a) Identify the attribute best suitable to be declared as a primary key. 1

(b) Write the degree and cardinality of the table STORE. 1

(c) Insert the following data into the attributes ItemNo, ItemName and SCode respectively in the given table STORE. 1

ItemNo = 2010, ItemName = "Note Book" and Scode = 25

(d) Abhay want to remove the table STORE from the database MyStore. 1

Which command will he use from the following:

(a) DELETE FROM store;

(b) DROP TABLE store;

(c) DROP DATABASE mystore;

(d) DELETE store FROM mystore;

(e) Now Abhay wants to display the structure of the table STORE, i.e, name of the attributes and their respective data types that he has used in the table. Write the query to display the same. 1

23. Ranjan Kumar of class 12 is writing a program to create a CSV file "user.csv" which will contain user name and password for some entries. He has written the following code. As a programmer, help him to successfully execute the given task.

```
import__________                                        # Line 1

def addCsvFile(UserName,PassWord):   # to write / add data into the CSV
file
    f=open(' user.csv','__________')                    # Line 2
    newFileWriter = csv.writer(f)
    newFileWriter.writerow([UserName,PassWord])
    f.close()

#csv file reading code
def readCsvFile():          # to read data from CSV file
    with open(' user.csv','r') as newFile:
        newFileReader = csv.__________(newFile)         # Line 3
        for row in newFileReader:
            print (row[0],row[1])
    newFile.__________                                  # Line 4

addCsvFile("Arjun","123@456")
addCsvFile("Arunima","aru@nima")
addCsvFile("Frieda","myname@FRD")
readCsvFile()                                           #Line 5
```

(a) Name the module he should import in Line 1. 1

(b) In which mode, Ranjan should open the file to add data into the file. 1

(c) Fill in the blank in Line 3 to read the data from a csv file. 1

(d) Fill in the blank in Line 4 to close the file. 1

(e) Write the output he will obtain while executing Line 5. 1

PART - B

SECTION – I

Each question carries 2 marks **(2 × 10 = 20)**

24. Evaluate the following expressions: 2

(a) 6 * 3 + 4**2 // 5 – 8 (b) 10 > 5 and 7 > 12 or not 18 > 3

25. Differentiate between Viruses and Worms in context of networking and data communication threats. 2

OR

Differentiate between Web server and Web browser. Write any two popular Web browsers.

26. Expand the following terms: 2

(a) SMTP (b) XML (c) LAN (d) IPR

27. Differentiate between actual parameter(s) and a formal parameter(s) with a suitable example for each. 2

OR

Explain the use of global keyword used in a function with the help of a suitable example.

28. Rewrite the following code in Python after removing all syntax error(s). 2

Underline each correction done in the code.

```
Value=30
for VAL in range(0,Value)
    If val%4==0:
        print (VAL*4)
    Elseif val%5==0:
        print (VAL+3)
    else
        print(VAL+10)
```

29. What possible outputs(s) are expected to be displayed on screen at the time of execution of the program from the following code? Also specify the maximum values that can be assigned to each of the variables Lower and Upper. 2

```
import random
AR=[20,30,40,50,60,70];
```

```
Lower =random.randint(1,3)
Upper =random.randint(2,4)
for K in range(Lower, Upper +1):
    print (AR[K],end="#")
```

(a) 10#40#70#   (b) 30#40#50#   (c) 50#60#70#   (d) 40#50#70#

30. What do you understand by Candidate Keys in a table? Give a suitable example of Candidate Keys from a table containing some meaningful data. 2

31. Differentiate between fetchone() and fetchall() methods with suitable examples for each. 2

32. Write the full forms of DDL and DML. Write any two commands of DML in SQL. 2

33. Find and write the output of the following Python code: 2

```
def Display(str):
    m=""
    for i in range(0,len(str)):
        if(str[i].isupper()):
            m=m+str[i].lower()
        elif str[i].islower():
            m=m+str[i].upper()
        else:
            if i%2==0:
                m=m+str[i-1]
            else:
                m=m+"#"
    print(m)

Display('Fun@Python3.0')
```

SECTION – II

Each question carries 3 marks **(3 × 4 = 12)**

34. Write a function LShift(Arr,n) in Python, which accepts a list Arr of numbers and n is a numeric value by which all elements of the list are shifted to left. 3

Sample Input Data of the list

```
Arr= [ 10,20,30,40,12,11], n=2
```

```
Output
Arr = [30,40,12,11,10,20]
```

35. Write a function in Python that counts the number of "Me" or "My" words present in a text file "STORY.TXT". 3

If the "STORY.TXT" contents are as follows:

My first book

was Me and

My Family. It

gave me

chance to be

Known to the

world.

The output of the function should be:

Count of Me/My in file: 4

OR

Write a function AMCount() in Python, which should read each character of a text file STORY.TXT, should count and display the occurance of alphabets A and M (including small cases a and m too).

Example:

If the file content is as follows:

Updated information

As simplified by official websites.

The EUCount() function should display the output as:

A or a:4

M or m :2

36. Write the outputs of the SQL queries (a) to (c) based on the relations Teacher and Posting given below: 3

Table : Teacher						
T_ID	**Name**	**Age**	**Department**	**Date_of_join**	**Salary**	**Gender**
1	Jugal	34	Computer Sc	10/01/2017	12000	M
2	Sharmila	31	History	24/03/2008	20000	F
3	Sandeep	32	Mathematics	12/12/2016	30000	M
4	Sangeeta	35	History	01/07/2015	40000	F

5	Rakesh	42	Mathematics	05/09/2007	25000	M
6	Shyam	50	History	27/06/2008	30000	M
7	Shiv Om	44	Computer Sc	25/02/2017	21000	M
8	Shalakha	33	Mathematics	31/07/2018	20000	F

Table : Posting

P_ID	Department	Place
1	History	Agra
2	Mathematics	Raipur
3	Computer Science	Delhi

(a) SELECT Department, count(*) FROM Teacher
GROUP BY Department;

(b) SELECT Max(Date_of_Join),Min(Date_of_Join) FROM Teacher;

(c) SELECT Teacher.name, Teacher.Department, Posting.Place FROM Teacher, Posting WHERE Teacher.Department = Posting.Department AND Posting. Place="Delhi";

37. Write a function in Python PUSH(Arr), where Arr is a list of numbers. From this list push all numbers divisible by 5 into a stack implemented by using a list. Display the stack if it has at least one element, otherwise display appropriate error message. 3

OR

Write a function in Python POP(Arr), where Arr is a stack implemented by a list of numbers. The function returns the value deleted from the stack.

SECTION – III

Each question carries 5 marks **(5 × 3 = 15)**

38. MyPace University is setting up its academic blocks at Naya Raipur and is planning to set up a network. The University has 3 academic blocks and one Human Resource Center as shown in the diagram below: 5

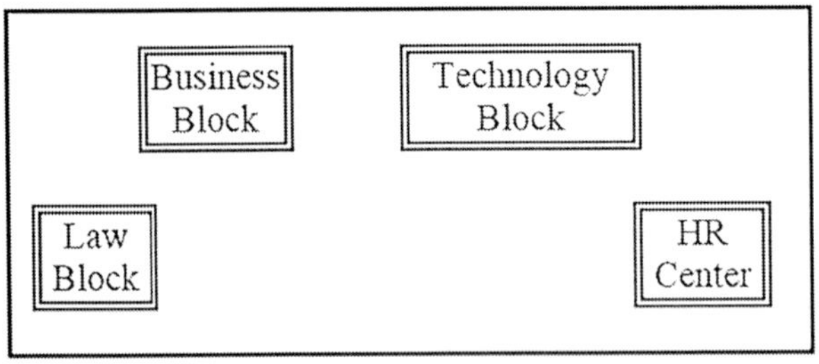

Center to Center distances between various blocks/center is as follows:

Law Block to business Block	40m
Law block to Technology Block	80m
Law Block to HR center	105m
Business Block to technology Block	30m
Business Block to HR Center	35m
Technology block to HR center	15m

Number of computers in each of the blocks/Center is as follows:

Law Block	15
Technology Block	40
HR center	115
Business Block	25

(a) Suggest the most suitable place (i.e., Block/Center) to install the server of this University with a suitable reason.

(b) Suggest an ideal layout for connecting these blocks/centers for a wired connectivity.

(c) Which device will you suggest to be placed/installed in each of these blocks/centers to efficiently connect all the computers within these blocks/centers.

(d) Suggest the placement of a Repeater in the network with justification.

(e) The university is planning to connect its admission office in Delhi, which is more than 1250 km from university. Which type of network out of LAN, MAN, or WAN will be formed? Justify your answer.

39. Write SQL commands for the following queries (a) to (e) based on the relations Teacher and Posting given below: 5

Table : Teacher

T_ID	Name	Age	Department	Date_of_join	Salary	Gender
1	Jugal	34	Computer Sc	10/01/2017	12000	M
2	Sharmila	31	History	24/03/2008	20000	F
3	Sandeep	32	Mathematics	12/12/2016	30000	M
4	Sangeeta	35	History	01/07/2015	40000	F
5	Rakesh	42	Mathematics	05/09/2007	25000	M
6	Shyam	50	History	27/06/2008	30000	M
7	Shiv Om	44	Computer Sc	25/02/2017	21000	M
8	Shalakha	33	Mathematics	31/07/2018	20000	F

Table : Posting		
P_ID	**Department**	**Place**
1	History	Agra
2	Mathematics	Raipur
3	Computer Science	Delhi

(a) To show all information about the teacher of History department.

(b) To list the names of female teachers who are in Mathematics department.

(c) To list the names of all teachers with their date of joining in ascending order.

(d) To display teacher's name, salary, age for male teachers only.

(e) To display name, bonus for each teacher where bonus is 10% of salary.

40. A binary file "Book.dat" has structure [BookNo, Book_Name, Author, Price]. 5

(a) Write a user defined function CreateFile() to input data for a record and add to Book.dat .

(b) Write a function CountRec(Author) in Python which accepts the Author name as parameter and count and return number of books by the given Author are stored in the binary file "Book.dat"

OR

A binary file "STUDENT.DAT" has structure (admission_number, Name, Percentage). Write a function countrec() in Python that would read contents of the file "STUDENT.DAT" and display the details of those students whose percentage is above 75. Also display number of students scoring above 75%.

Answers

PART – A

SECTION – I

1. (b) True

   (c) 2ndName

   ½ mark for mentioning each correct invalid identifier

2. [6,82,5] 1 mark for giving the correct output

3. Comma Separated Value ' 1 mark for writing the correct full form

4. (c) ** 1 mark for mentioning the valid arithmetic operator from the list given

5. (b) T[2]= -29 (as tuple is immutable)

   1 mark for choosing the correct statement from the given options

6. Day={1:'Monday', 2:'Tuesday', 3:'Wednesday'}

   1 mark for writing the correct Python statement for declaring dictionary

7. 30 1 mark for the correct output

8. abs() 1 mark for naming the correct built-in function

9. SMTP / Simple Mail Transfer Protocol

   1 mark for writing the correct name of the protocol

10. Identity Theft 1 mark for mentioning the correct type of cybercrime

11. ORDER BY

    1 mark for mentioning the correct clause for displaying the tuples in ascending order

12. To check if the column has null value / no value

    1 mark for mentioning the correct use of IS NULL operator

13. SUM / AVG / COUNT / MAX / MIN

    1 mark for mentioning any one aggregate function

14. (b) ALTER 1 mark for choosing the correct DDL command from the options given.

15. Microwave / Radio wave

    1 mark for mentioning any one correct transmission media for connecting to hilly areas

16. (d) List 1 mark for correct identification of the given declaration.

17. puterSc 1 mark for writing the correct output

18. SHOW TABLES

    1 mark for the correct SQL statement to display the tables in the database.

19. Wireless Fidelity 1 mark for the correct full form

20. (c) Primary Key 1 mark for choosing the correct type of table constraint

21. Bps, Kbps, Mbps, Gbps, Tbps 1 mark for writing the given terms in increasing order

SECTION – II

22. (a) ItemNo is best suitable to be declared as a primary key.

1 mark for writing the appropriate primary key

(b) Degree = 4 Cardinality = 7

½ mark each for writing the correct degree and cardinality

(c) INSERT INTO store (ItemNo, ItemName, Scode) VALUES(2010, "Note Book", 25);

½ mark for INSERT INTO store ItemNo, ItemName, Scode) and
½ mark for VALUES(2010, "Note Book", 25);

(d) DROP TABLE store; 1 mark for choosing the correct statement for removing the table

(e) Describe Store; OR DESC Store;

1 mark for the correct query to display the structure of the table.

23. (a) Line 1 : csv 1 mark for writing csv

(b) Ranjan should open the file in append mode ('a') so Line 2 : a

1 mark for mentioning append more or just writing 'a'

(c) Line 3 : reader 1 mark for the reader

(d) Line 4 : close() 1 mark for close()

(e) Output while executing Line 5

Arjun 123@456

Arunima aru@nima

Frieda myname@FRD 1 mark for the correct output

PART - B

SECTION – I

24. (a) 13

(b) False 1 mark for each correct output

25. Viruses require an active host program or an already-infected and active operating system in order for viruses to run, cause damage and infect other executable files or documents. Worms are stand-alone malicious programs that can self-replicate.

1 mark each for defining virus and worm

OR

Web Browser: A web browser is a software application for accessing information on the World Wide Web. When a user requests a web page from a particular website, the web browser retrieves the necessary content from a web server and then displays the page on the user's device.

Web Server: A web server is a computer that runs websites. The basic objective of the web server is to store, process and deliver web pages to the users. This intercommunication is done using Hypertext Transfer Protocol (HTTP).

Popular web browsers: Google Chrome, Mozilla Firefox, Internet Explorer etc

1 mark for any correct difference between web browser and web server.
½ mark each for naming any web browser correctly.

26. (a) SMTP: Simple Mail Transfer Protocol
(b) XML: eXtensible Markup Language
(c) LAN: Local Area Network
(d) IPR: Intellectual Property Rights

½ mark for each correct full form.

27. The list of identifiers used in a function call is called actual parameter(s) whereas the list of parameters used in the function definition is called formal parameter(s).

Actual parameter may be value/ variable or expression.

Formal parameter is an identifier.

Example:

```
def area(side):          # line 1
    return side*side;
print(area(5))           # line 2
```

In line 1, side is the formal parameter and in line 2, while invoking area() function, the value 5 is the actual parameter.

A formal parameter, i.e. a parameter, is in the function definition. An actual parameter, i.e. an argument, is in a function call.

1 mark for any correct difference between actual parameter(s) and formal parameter(s).
1 mark for any correct example

OR

Use of global keyword:

In Python, global keyword allows the programmer to modify the variable outside the current scope. It is used to create a global variable and make changes to the variable in local context. A variable declared inside a function is by default local and a variable declared outside the function is global by default. The keyword global is written inside the function to use its global value. Outside the function, global keyword has no effect.

Example:

```
c = 10 # global variable def add():  global c  c = c + 2
```

```
# global value of c is incremented by 2
print("Inside add():", c)

add() c=15
print("In main:", c)

output:
Inside add() : 12
In main: 15
```

1 mark for writing any correct use of global keyword used in the function
1 mark for mentioning the example.

28. CORRECTED CODE:

```
Value=30
for VAL in range(0,Value) :          # Error 1 - colon missing
    if VAL%4==0:                     # Error 2 - If and val
        print (VAL*4)
    elif VAL%5==0:                   # Error 3 - Elseif and val
        print (VAL+3)
    else:                            # Error 4 – colon missing
        print(VAL+10)
```

½ mark for mentioning and correcting each error in the code

29. OUTPUT: (b)

Maximum value of Lower: 3

Maximum value of Upper: 4

1 mark for choosing the correct output from the options given
½ mark each for writing the maximum value of lower and upper

30. A table may have more than one such attribute / group of attributes that identifies a tuple uniquely, all such attribute(s) are known as Candidate Keys.

Table: Item		
Ino	**Item**	**Qty**
I01	Pen	500
I02	Pencil	700
I04	CD	500
I09		700
I05	Eraser	300
I03	Duster	200

In the above table Item, ItemNo can be a candidate key

1 mark for defining candidate key
1 mark for any correct example for explaining candidate keys

31. **fetchall()** fetches all the rows of a query result. An empty list is returned if there is no record to fetch the cursor.

fetchone() method returns one row or a single record at a time. It will return None if no more rows / records are available.

Example for fetchall():

```
import mysql.connector
mydb = mysql.connector.connect(host="localhost", user="root", pass-
wd="root", database="School")
mycur=mydb.cursor()
s="SELECT * FROM Teacher"
mycur.execute(s)
result=mycur.fetchall()
for a in result:
   print(a)
print(mycur.rowcount," total records in the table")
```

Example for fetchone():

```
import mysql.connector
mydb = mysql.connector.connect(host="localhost", user="root", pass-
wd="root", database="School")
mycur=mydb.cursor()
s="SELECT * FROM Teacher"
mycur.execute(s)
result=mycur.fetchone()
print(result)
```

1 mark for any correct difference between fetchall() and fetchone()
1 mark for any correct example

32. DDL: Data Definition Language

DML: Data Manipulation Language

Any two out of INSERT, DELETE, UPDATE

½ mark each for correct full form of DDL and DML
½ mark each for writing any correct DML statement/ command

33. OUTPUT : **fUN#pYTHONn#.**

½ mark for adding the lowercase characters as uppercase characters
½ mark for adding uppercase characters as lowercase characters
½ mark for adding the even locations with the previous character
½ mark for adding the odd locations with a # symbol

SECTION – II

34.
```
def LShift(Arr,n):
    L=len(Arr)
    for x in range(0,n):
        y=Arr[0]
        for i in range(0,L-1):
            Arr[i]=Arr[i+1]
        Arr[L-1]=y
    print(Arr)
```

OR

```
def LShift(Arr, n):
    for i in range(n):
        temp=Arr[0]
        for j in range(len(Arr)-1):
            Arr[j]=Arr[j+1]
        Arr[j+1]=temp
        print(Arr)

LShift([10,20,30,40,12,11], 2)
```

Note: Using of any correct code giving the same result is also accepted.

35.
```
def displayMeMy():
    num=0
    f=open("story.txt","r")
    N=f.read()
    for x in N.split():
        if x=="Me" or x== "My":
            num=num+1
    f.close()
    print("Count of Me/My in file:",num)
```

OR

```
def AMCount():
    try:
        with open('story.txt','r') as fin:
            ch=fin.read()
            print(ch)
            ctra,ctrm=0,0
            for i in ch:
                if i in ['a','A']:
                    ctra+=1
                elif i in ['m','M']:
                    ctrm+=1
            print("A or a: ",ctra)
            print("M or m: ",ctrm)
    except FileNotFoundError:
        print("File not found")
AMCount()
```

Note: Using of any correct code giving the same result is also accepted.

36. OUTPUT:

(a)

Department	Count(*)
History	3
Computer Sc	2
Mathematics	3

(b) Max - 31/07/2018 or 2018-07-31 Min- 05/09/2007 or 2007-09-05

(c)

name	Department	Place
Jugal	Computer Sc	Delhi
Shiv Om	Computer Sc	Delhi

1 mark for each correct output

37. ANSWER: (Using of any correct code giving the same result is also accepted.)

```
def PUSH(Arr, value):
    s=[]
    for x in range(0, len(Arr)):
        if Arr[x]%5==0:
            s.append(Arr[x])
```

```
    if len(s)==0:
        print("Empty Stack")      else:
    print(s)
```

OR

```
def popStack(st) :
# If stack is empty
    if len(st)==0:
        print("Underflow")
    else:
        L = len(st)
        val=st[L-1]
        print(val)
        st.pop(L-1)
```

SECTION – III

38. (a) Most suitable place to install the server is HR center, as this center has maximum number of computers.

½ mark for suggesting the most suitable place to install the server and ½ mark for mentioning the reason

(b) Star Topology

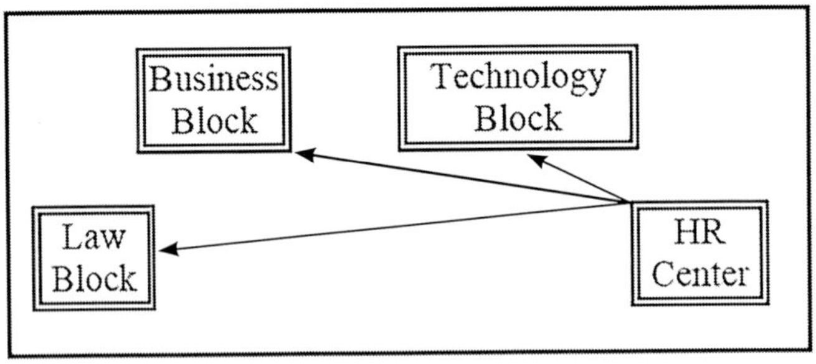

½ mark for drawing the layout and ½ mark for mentioning the layout

(c) Hub/ Switch

1 mark for mentioning any of the device hub/switch

(d) Repeater may be placed when the distance between 2 buildings is more than 70 meter.

½ mark for mentioning the correct placement of repeater and ½ mark for justification

WAN, as the given distance is more than the range of LAN and MAN.

½ mark for mentioning WAN and ½ mark for any valid justification

39. (a) SELECT * FROM teacher
WHERE department= "History";

½ mark for SELECT statement and ½ mark for the second part of the SQL query

(b) SELECT name FROM teacher
WHERE department= "Mathematics" AND gender= "F";

½ mark for the first part of the query and ½ mark for the second part of the query

(c) SELECT name FROM teacher
ORDER BY date_of_join;

½ mark for the first part of the query and ½ mark for the second part of the query

(d) SELECT name, salary, age FROM teacher
WHERE gender='M';

½ mark for the first part of the query and ½ mark for the second part of the query

(e) SELECT name, salary*0.1 AS Bonus FROM teacher;

1 mark for the correct SQL query

40. ANSWER: (Using of any correct code giving the same result is also accepted.)

```
import pickle

def createFile():
    fobj=open("Book.dat","ab")
    BookNo=int(input("Book Number : "))
    Book_name=input("Name :")
    Author = input("Author: ")
    Price = int(input("Price  : "))
    rec=[BookNo,Book_Name,Author,Price]
    pickle.dump(rec,fobj)
    fobj.close()

def CountRec(Author):
    fobj=open("Book.dat","rb")
    num = 0
    try:
        while True:
            rec=pickle.load(fobj)
            if Author==rec[2]:
                num = num + 1
```

```
    except:
        fobj.close()
    return num
```

OR

```
import pickle

def CountRec():
with open("STUDENT.DAT","rb") as fobj:
    num = 0
    try:
        while True:
            rec=pickle.load(fobj)
            if rec[2] > 75:
                print(rec[0], rec[1], rec[2], sep="\t")
                num = num + 1
    except:
        fobj.close()
    return num
```

Extra Bytes

Python

Check which version of python is installed in your device by entering the following command in the command prompt:

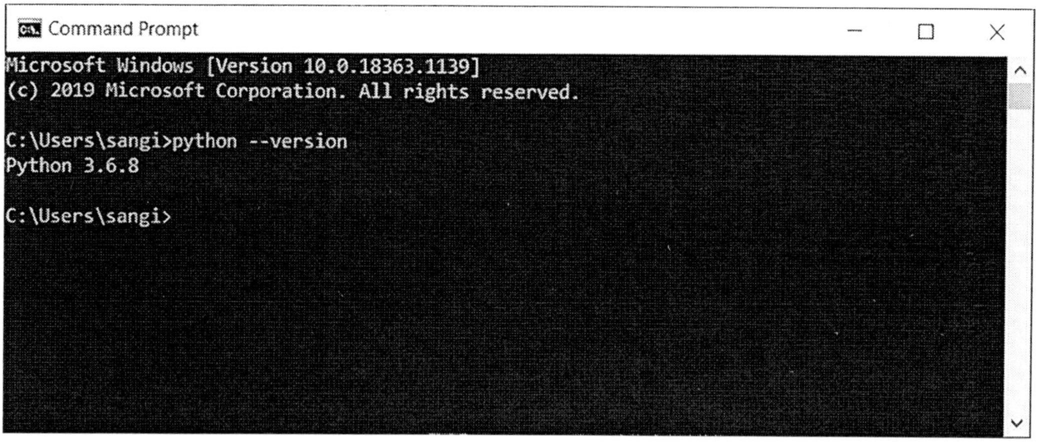

Tkinter & Python

- It is a package/ library in Python to create **Graphical User Interface (GUI)**.
- It provides object-oriented interface. To work with Tkinter in python, we need to first install it by using the pip install Tkinter command and then use the following statement in python code to use it:

  from Tkinter import *
- We can use different widgets like label, textbox, combobox, buttons to make it interactive.
- Geometry managers are used for the layout of the window.
- Buttons play very important role to make it interactive so as to invoke the functionality as per the button click.

MySQL & Python

- MySQL is an open source **RDBMS (Relational Database Management System**.
- It is used to create and manage data in the form of records in the form of a table known as relation.
- Python requires MySQL driver to access the MySQL database.
- Install MySQL connector by using the following command:

  pip install mysql-connecctor-python
- To use MySQL in the python code, following command is used:

  import mysql.connector

SAMPLE PROJECT

Sample Output screens

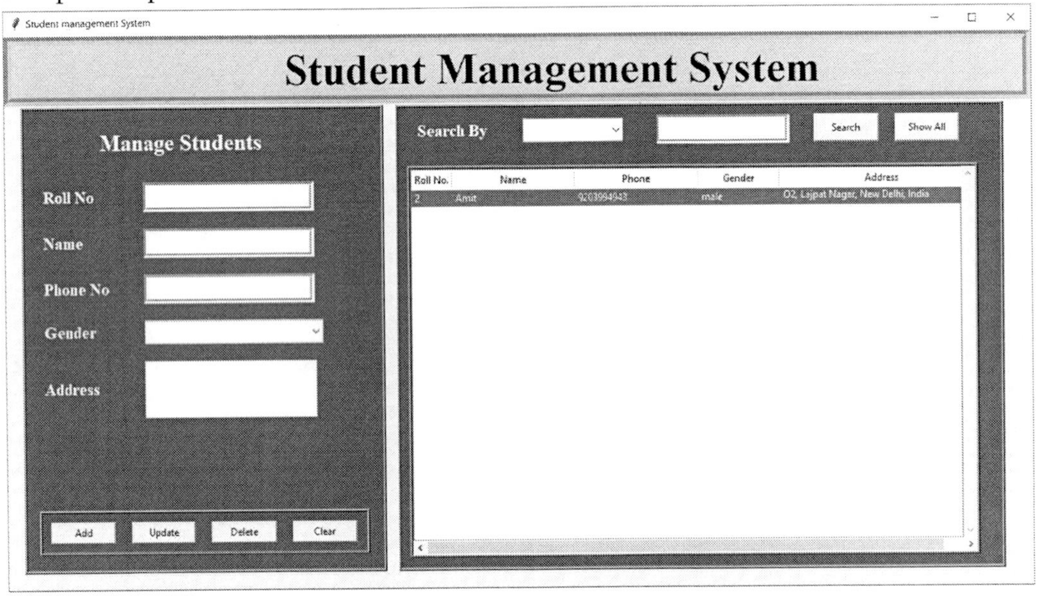


```
from tkinter import *
from tkinter import ttk
import pymysql
from tkinter import messagebox

class Student:
    def __init__(self, root):
        self.root=root
        self.root.title("Student management System")
        self.root.geometry("1350x700+0+0")

        title=Label(self.root, text="Student Management System",bd=10, relief=GROOVE, font=("times new roman",40, "bold"),bg="yellow")
        title.pack(side=TOP, fill=X)

        #Variables
        self.Roll_No_var=StringVar()
        self.name_var=StringVar()
        self.phone_var=StringVar()
```

```
self.gender_var=StringVar()
self.address_var=StringVar()

self.search_by=StringVar()
self.search_text=StringVar()

# Managing frame

Manage_Frame=Frame(self.root, bd=4, relief=RIDGE, bg="crimson")
Manage_Frame.place(x=20, y=85, width=450, height=560)
m_title=Label(Manage_Frame, text="Manage Students", bg="crimson", fg="white", font=("times new roman",20, "bold"))
m_title.grid(row=0, columnspan=2, pady=20)

lbl_roll=Label(Manage_Frame, text="Roll No", bg="crimson", fg="white", font=("times new roman",15, "bold"))
lbl_roll.grid(row=1, column=0, pady=10, padx=20, sticky="w")
txt_Roll=Entry(Manage_Frame, textvariable=self.Roll_No_var, font=("times new roman",15, "bold"), bd=5, relief=GROOVE)
txt_Roll.grid(row=1, column=1, pady=10, padx=20, sticky="w")

lbl_name=Label(Manage_Frame,text="Name", bg="crimson", fg="white", font=("times new roman",15, "bold"))
lbl_name.grid(row=2, column=0, pady=10, padx=20, sticky="w")
txt_Name=Entry(Manage_Frame, textvariable=self.name_var, font=("-times new roman",15, "bold"), bd=5, relief=GROOVE)
txt_Name.grid(row=2, column=1, pady=10, padx=20, sticky="w")

lbl_Phone=Label(Manage_Frame, text="Phone No", bg="crimson", fg="white", font=("times new roman",15, "bold"))
lbl_Phone.grid(row=3, column=0, pady=10, padx=20, sticky="w")
txt_Phone=Entry(Manage_Frame, textvariable=self.phone_var, font=("times new roman",15, "bold"), bd=5, relief=GROOVE)
txt_Phone.grid(row=3, column=1, pady=10, padx=20, sticky="w")

lbl_Gender=Label(Manage_Frame, text="Gender", bg="crimson", fg="white", font=("times new roman",15, "bold"))
```

```
    lbl_Gender.grid(row=4, column=0, pady=10, padx=20, sticky="w")

    combo_gender=ttk.Combobox(Manage_Frame, textvariable=self.gen-
    der_var, font=("times new roman",15, "bold"), state="readonly")
    combo_gender['values']=("Male","Female","Other")
    combo_gender.grid(row=4, column=1, padx=20, pady=10)

    lbl_Address=Label(Manage_Frame, text="Address", bg="crimson",
    fg="white", font=("times new roman",15, "bold"))
    lbl_Address.grid(row=5, column=0, pady=10, padx=20, sticky="w")

    self.txt_Address=Text(Manage_Frame, width=30, height=4,
    font=("",10))
    self.txt_Address.grid(row=5, column=1, padx=20, pady=10,
    sticky="w")

#button frame

    btn_Frame=Frame(Manage_Frame, bd=4, relief=RIDGE, bg="crimson")
    btn_Frame.place(x=15, y=480, width=410)

    Addbtn=Button(btn_Frame, text="Add", width=10, command=self.add_
    student).grid(row=0,column=0, padx=10, pady=10)
    updatebtn=Button(btn_Frame, text="Update", width=10, command=self.
    update_data).grid(row=0,column=1, padx=10, pady=10)
    deletebtn=Button(btn_Frame, text="Delete", width=10, command=self.
    delete_data).grid(row=0,column=2, padx=10, pady=10)
    Clearbtn=Button(btn_Frame, text="Clear", width=10, command=self.
    clear).grid(row=0,column=3, padx=10, pady=10)

    Detail_Frame=Frame(self.root, bd=4, relief=RIDGE, bg="crimson")
    Detail_Frame.place(x=500, y=85, width=800, height=560)

    lbl_search= Label(Detail_Frame, text="Search By", bg="crimson",
    fg="white", font=("times new roman",15, "bold"))
    lbl_search.grid(row=0, column=0, pady=10, padx=20, sticky="w")

    combo_search=ttk.Combobox(Detail_Frame,textvariable=self.search_
```

```
by, width=10, font=("times new roman",15, "bold"), state="readon-
ly")
combo_search['values']=("roll_no","name","phone")
combo_search.grid(row=0, column=1, padx=20, pady=10)

txt_Search=Entry(Detail_Frame,textvariable=self.search_text,
width=15,font=("times new roman",15, "bold"), bd=5, relief=GROOVE)
txt_Search.grid(row=0, column=2, pady=10, padx=20, sticky="w")

searchbt=Button(Detail_Frame, text="Search", width=10, pady=5, com-
mand=self.search_data).grid(row=0, column=3, padx=10, pady=10)
showallbtn=Button(Detail_Frame, text="Show All", width=10, pady=5,
command=self.display_data).grid(row=0, column=4, padx=10, pady=10)

#Table frame

Table_Frame=Frame(Detail_Frame, bd=4, relief=RIDGE, bg="crimson")
Table_Frame.place(x=10, y=70, width=700, height=470)

scroll_x=Scrollbar(Table_Frame, orient=HORIZONTAL)
scroll_y=Scrollbar(Table_Frame, orient=VERTICAL)

self.Student_table=ttk.Treeview(Table_Frame, columns=("roll","name",
"phone","gender","address"), xscrollcommand=scroll_x.set,yscroll-
command=scroll_y.set)

scroll_x.pack(side=BOTTOM, fill=X)
scroll_y.pack(side=RIGHT, fill=Y)

scroll_x.config(command=self.Student_table.xview)
scroll_y.config(command=self.Student_table.yview)

self.Student_table.heading("roll", text="Roll No.")
self.Student_table.heading("name", text="Name")
self.Student_table.heading("phone", text="Phone")
self.Student_table.heading("gender", text="Gender")
self.Student_table.heading("address", text="Address")
```

```
        self.Student_table['show']='headings'

        self.Student_table.column("roll", width=50)
        self.Student_table.column("name", width=150)
        self.Student_table.column("phone", width=150)
        self.Student_table.column("gender", width=100)
        self.Student_table.column("address", width=250)

        self.Student_table.pack(fill=BOTH, expand=1)
        self.Student_table.bind("<ButtonRelease-1>", self.get_data)
        self.display_data()

    def add_student(self):
        if self.Roll_No_var.get()=="" or self.name_var.get()=="":
            messagebox.showerror("Error","All fields are required")
        else:
            con=pymysql.connect(host="localhost", user="root", password="-
            root", database="stm")
            cur=con.cursor()
            cur.execute("insert into students values(%s, %s, %s, %s, %s)",
            (self.Roll_No_var.get(),
            self.name_var.get(),
            self.phone_var.get(),
            self.gender_var.get(),
            self.txt_Address.get('1.0',END)
            ))
            con.commit()
            con.close()
            self.display_data()
            self.clear()
            messagebox.showinfo("Success","Record has inserted")

    def display_data(self):
        con=pymysql.connect(host="localhost", user="root", password="-
        root", database="stm")
```

```
        cur=con.cursor()
        cur.execute("select * from students")
        rows=cur.fetchall()
        if len(rows)!=0:
            self.Student_table.delete(*self.Student_table.get_children())
            for row in rows:
                self.Student_table.insert('',END,values=row)
            con.commit()
        con.close()

    def clear(self):
        self.Roll_No_var.set("")
        self.name_var.set("")
        self.phone_var.set("")
        self.gender_var.set("")
        self.txt_Address.delete("1.0",END)

    def get_data(self, ev):
        cursor_row=self.Student_table.focus()
        contents=self.Student_table.item(cursor_row)
        row=contents['values']
        self.Roll_No_var.set(row[0])
        self.name_var.set(row[1])
        self.phone_var.set(row[2])
        self.gender_var.set(row[3])
        self.txt_Address.delete('1.0',END)
        self.txt_Address.insert(END, row[4])

    def update_data(self):
        con=pymysql.connect(host="localhost", user="root", password="-
        root", database="stm")
        cur=con.cursor()
        cur.execute("update students set name=%s, phone=%s, gender=%s, ad-
        dress=%s where roll_no=%s",
        (self.name_var.get(),
        self.phone_var.get(),
```

```
        self.gender_var.get(),
        self.txt_Address.get('1.0',END),
        self.Roll_No_var.get()
        ))
        con.commit()
        con.close()
        self.display_data()
        self.clear()

    def delete_data(self):
        con=pymysql.connect(host="localhost", user="root", password="-
        root", database="stm")
        cur=con.cursor()
        cur.execute("delete from students where roll_no=%s",self.Roll_No_
        var.get())
        con.commit()
        con.close()
        self.display_data()
        self.clear()

    def search_data(self):
        con=pymysql.connect(host="localhost", user="root", password="-
        root", database="stm")
        cur=con.cursor()
        cur.execute("select * from students where "+ str(self.search_
        by.get())+" LIKE '%"+str(self.search_text.get())+"%'")
        rows=cur.fetchall()
        if len(rows)!=0:
            self.Student_table.delete(*self.Student_table.get_children())
            for row in rows:
                self.Student_table.insert('',END,values=row)
            con.commit()
        con.close()

root=Tk()
ob=Student(root)
root.mainloop()
```

Solved Sample Papers

Computer Science (083)

Solved Sample Paper – 1 (Theory)

M.M.: 70 **Time: 3 hrs**

General Instructions

1. This question paper contains two parts A and B. Each part is compulsory.
2. Both Part A and Part B have choices.
3. Part-A has 2 sections:
   a. Section – I is short answer questions, to be answered in one word or one line.
   b. Section – II has two case studies questions. Each case study has 4 case-based subparts. An examinee is to attempt any 4 out of the 5 subparts.
4. Part - B is Descriptive Paper.
5. Part- B has three sections
   a. Section-I is short answer questions of 2 marks each in which two question have internal options.
   b. Section-II is long answer questions of 3 marks each in which two questions have internal options.
   c. Section-III is very long answer questions of 5 marks each in which one question has internal option.
6. All programming questions are to be answered using Python Language only.

PART - A

SECTION – I

Attempt any 15 questions from question numbers 1 to 21. Each question carries 1 mark. **(1 × 15 = 15 marks)**

1. Out of the following, which all can be considered as valid names for identifiers in Python: 1

   (a) For (b) 12A (c) First Name (d) age

2. Given the following list: 1

   L1 = [1, "Abhay", [87, 90, 95, 76, 45]]

   Write the output of the following statement:

   print(L1 [2])

3. Write any two file modes while working with external files (File handling) in Python. 1

4. Which one of the following is not a part of token in Python? 1

(a) Delimiter (b) Identifiers (c) Keywords (d) Functions

5. Identify the valid relational operator in Python from the following: 1

(a) or (b) ** (c) && (d) !=

6. Write a statement in Python to declare a list having values 301, 041, 042, 043, 083 and another list within it having values English, Mathematics, Physics, Chemistry and Computer Science. 1

7. A tuple is declared as: 1

T1 = (10, 20, 12, 5, 8, 11)

What will be the output of the following statement?

print(sum(T1) / len(T1))

8. Name the Python Library module which need to be imported to use the pow() and load() function. 1

9. Name the protocol used for uploading and downloading the files. 1

10. Name the type of cyber threat / cyber activity in which a person keeps track or harass another person by misusing the Internet. 1

11. In SQL, name the clause and the keyword which is used to display the tuples in descending order of an attribute. 1

12. In SQL, name the operator which is used for pattern matching. 1

13. Write any one multiple row function (group functions) used in SQL. 1

14. Choose the DDL commands from the following: 1

(a) SELECT (b) ALTER (c) INSERT (d) DROP

15. Name the transmission media which consists of two insulated copper wires that are twisted together in a helical form. 1

16. Write any one difference between List and Tuple. 1

17. Write the output of the following code: 1

str = "Programming with Python is fun"

print(str[::-1])

18. In SQL, write the query to display the list of databases stored in SQL. 1

19. Write the expanded form of ARPANET. 1

20. Write any one difference between Unique and Primary key constraint. 1

21. Define bandwidth in data communication. Also, write the unit for measuring the bandwidth. 1

SECTION – II

Consists of case study questions and are compulsory to attempt. Attempt any 4 sub parts from each question. Each sub part carries 1 mark. (4 + 4 = 8 marks)

22. A school named Modern is trying to maintain their employee's details using SQL to store the data for an inventory. As a database admin, Aryan has decided to declare the following to create the inventory:

- Name of the database: School
- Name of the table: Teacher
- The attributes of Teacher are:

  T_ID: character of size 3

  Name: character of size 15

  Dept_ID: character of size 3

  Salary: numeric value of 6 digits

  Gender: character of size 1

Table: Teacher				
T_ID	Name	Dept_ID	Salary	Gender
100	Satish	041	70000	M
101	Jyotika	041	55000	F
102	Prabhjot	301	53000	F
103	Sudhanshu	042	85000	M
104	Sandeep	301	78000	M
105	Mohan	041	65000	M

(a) Identify the attribute best suitable to be declared as primary key. 1

(b) Write the degree and cardinality of the table Teacher. 1

(c) Insert the following data into the attributes T_ID, Name, Dept_ID and Salary respectively in the given table Teacher.

T_ID='106', Name='Sunita' and Dept_ID='301' 1

(d) Aryan wants to remove the records which are having Salary as NULL from the table Teacher. Which of the following command will he use to perform the task: 1

(i) DROP TABLE Teacher;

(ii) DELETE FROM Teacher WHERE Salary = NULL;

(iii) DELETE FROM Teacher WHERE Salary IS NULL;

(iv) DELETE Teacher FROM School;

(e) Aryan wants to display all the tables in the SCHOOL database. Write the query to display the same. 1

23. Abhay is writing a program to create a csv file "student.csv" which will contain the student id, name of the student and mobile number for all the students in their class. He has written the following code. As a programmer, help him to successfully execute the given code by fill in the blanks.

```
import______                          #Line 1

def add_student(admno, name, mobile):    #To add data to the CSV file
    with open('student.csv', '_', newline='') as fout:   #Line 2
        n=csv.writer(fout)
        n.writerow([admno, name, mobile])

def read_student():                               #to read data from CSV file
    with open('student.csv','r') as fin:
        n=csv.______(fin)                         #Line 3
        for r in n:
            print(__)                             #Line 4

add_student(1, "Aastha", 5566776611)
add_student(2, "Vasu", 8899001122)
add_student(3, "Charvi", 1100992211)
read_student()
```

(a) Name the module he should use with import statement in Line 1. 1

(b) In which mode, Abhay should open the file to keep adding more data to the CSV file. 1

(c) Fill in the blank in Line 3 to read the data from the CSV file. 1

(d) Fill in the blank in Line 4 to display the contents of the records read from the CSV file. 1

(e) Write the output of the program while executing the code. 1

PART – B

SECTION – I

Each question carries 2 marks **(2 × 10 = 20)**

24. Evaluate the following expressions: 2

(a) 3 + 6*4**2//3

(b) True and not(False) or False

25. Define Trojan horse and Spam. 2

OR

Write any two differences between HTML and XML.

26. Expand the following terms: 2

(a) SMTP (b) PAN (c) HTTPS (d) POP

27. What is the scope of the variable in functions? What are the two different types of variable scope in functions?

OR

Define Python built-in functions. How is it different from Python modules? 2

28. Rewrite the following code in python after removing all syntax error(s). Underline each correction done in the code. 2

```
10=A
input('Value of B: ', B)
if B>=A
    print(B-A)
    else:
    print(A-B)
```

29. What possible output(s) are expected to be displayed on screen at the time of execution of the program from the following code? Also, write the minimum and maximum value taken by x. 2

```
import random
List1=[2, 3, 4, 5, 6, 7]
From=random.randint(1,3)
To=random.randint(2,4)
for x in range(From, To+1):
    print(List1[x], end='#')
```

(a) 2#3# (b) 3#4#5# (c) 5#6#7# (d) 4#5#7#

30. Define primary key in a table. Give a suitable example of primary key from a table containing meaningful information. 2

31. What is the use of rowcount() method in SQL? Explain it with the help of a suitable example. 2

32. Define the use of DDL commands. Write any two DML commands in SQL. 2

33. Find and write the output of the following Python code: 2

```
def ChangeVal(A, B):
    for i in range(B):
        if A[i]%2 == 0:
            A[i] -= 3
        elif A[i]%3 == 0:
            A[i] /= 3
        else:
            A[i] *= 2

List1 = [4, 15, 8, 25]
ChangeVal(List1, 4)
for i in List1:
    print(i, end='@')
```

SECTION – II

Each question carries 3 marks **(3 × 4 = 12)**

34. Write a user defined function which accepts a list of integer elements and its size as argument. 3

The function divides all elements by 5 which are multiples of 5, divides the elements by 3 which are multiples of 3 and divides the elements by 2 which are multiples of 2 in the list.

Example:

If list passed is [20, 32, 10, 9, 15, 21, 12] and size = 7

Then the output of the code will be:

[5, 16, 2, 3, 3, 7, 4]

35. Write a function RevText() in Python to read a text file "input.txt" and print words starting with 'P' in reverse order else print the word in the same manner.

Example: If contents in text file is: PROGRAMMING WITH PYTHON IS FUN

Output will be: GNIMMARGORP WITH NOHTYP IS FUN 3

36. Write SQL commands for the following queries (a) to (c) based on the Table Teacher and Department given below: 3

Table: Teacher

T_ID	Name	Dept_ID	Salary	Gender
100	Satish	041	70000	M
101	Jyotika	041	55000	F
102	Prabhjot	301	53000	F
103	Sudhanshu	042	85000	M
104	Sandeep	301	78000	M
105	Mohan	041	65000	M

Table: Department	
Dept_ID	**Department**
301	English
041	Mathematics
042	Physics

(a) SELECT Department, SUM(Salary)
From Teacher T, Department D
WHERE T.Dept_ID=D.Dept_ID
GROUP BY T.Dept_ID;

(b) SELECT Gender, COUNT(*) FROM Teacher GROUP BY Gender;

(c) SELECT Name, Department, Salary
FROM Teacher T, Department D
WHERE T.Dept_ID=D.Dept_ID and Gender="M"
ORDER BY Name DESC;

37. Write a function in Python Push(S, Value) for performing Push operations on a Stack. Assuming the parameters S as a list and Value as an integer value for implementing the stack. Display the elements of the stack. 3

OR

Write a function in Python Pop(S) for performing Pop operations on list S as a Stack. Assuming the parameters S as a list for implementing the stack. Display the Stack after each Pop operation. Also, display an appropriate message when pop is invoked and there is no element in the stack.

SECTION – III

Each question carries 5 marks **(5 × 3 = 15)**

38. Aryan Private Limited is setting up its network in Hyderabad. There are four departments named Marketing, HR, Sales and Technical. 5

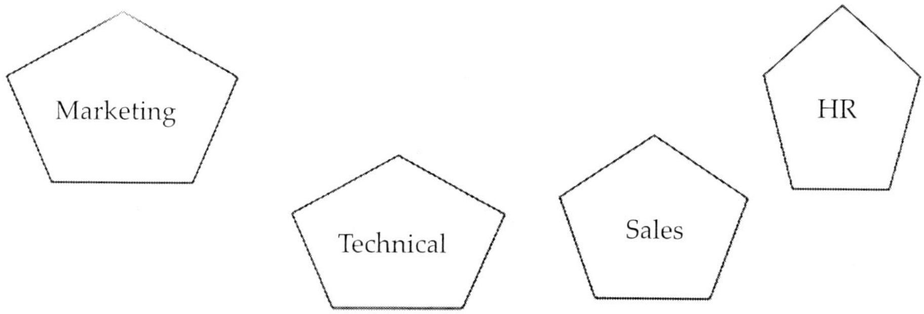

Distance between various buildings is given as follows:

Marketing to Technical	60 m
Sales to Technical	50 m
HR to Technical	110 m
Marketing to Sales	70 m
Marketing to HR	170 m
HR to Sales	70 m

Number of computers in each building:

Marketing	20
Technical	100
HR	25
Sales	30

(a) Suggest the cable layout of connections between the Departments and specify the topology.

(b) Suggest the most suitable building to place the server with a suitable reason.

(c) Which device will you suggest to be placed/ installed in each of these departments to efficiently connect all the computers within these departments?

(d) Suggest the placement of a Repeater in the network with justification.

(e) The organisation is planning to link its sale counter situated in various parts of the same city. Which type of network out of LAN, MAN, WAN will be formed? Justify your answer.

39. Write SQL commands for the following queries (a) to (e) based on the relations Teacher and Department given below: 5

Table: Teacher

T_ID	Name	Dept_ID	Salary	Gender
100	Satish	041	70000	M
101	Jyotika	041	55000	F
102	Prabhjot	301	53000	F
103	Sudhanshu	042	85000	M
104	Sandeep	301	78000	M
105	Mohan	041	65000	M

Table: Department	
Dept_ID	**Department**
301	English
041	Mathematics
042	Physics

(a) To show all the information of teachers from English department.

(b) To display the names of Male teachers who are in Mathematics department.

(c) To display the total number of teachers in each department.

(d) To change the Salary by giving 10% increment to all the employees of Mathematics department.

(e) To display Name, Department, Salary and Gender for Male teachers from table Teacher and Department.

40. A binary file "Emp.dat" has data in the following structure. 5

[Empno, Ename, Dept, Salary]

(a) Write a user defined function CreateEmp() in Python to accept the values for the record and add it to "Emp.dat".

(b) Write a user defined function Ctr_Rec(Department) in Python which accepts the Department as parameter, count and return the number of employees in the given department stored in the binary file "Emp.dat".

OR

A binary file "Bank.dat" has data in the following structure.
(Accno, Name, Ac_Type, Balance)

Write a function Check_Balance() in Python that would read contents of the file "Bank.dat" and display the details of those customers whose Balance is below 2000. Also, display the number of customers having balance below 2000.

Solved Sample Paper – 1 (Theory) - Answers

PART – A

SECTION – I

1. Valid names for identifiers in Python are: (a) For and (d) age

   ½ mark each for mentioning the valid name for identifier

2. [87, 90, 95, 76, 45]

   1 mark for the correct output

3. r / w / a / r+ / w+ / a+ / rb / wb / rb+ / wb+

   ½ mark for any correct file mode

4. (d) Functions

   1 mark for specifying functions

5. (d) != (not equal to)

   1 mark for correct identification of the relational operator

6. List1=['301', '041', '042', '043', '083', ['English', 'Mathematics', 'Physics', 'Chemistry', 'Computer Science']

   1 mark for correct statement to declare list

7. 11.0

   1 mark for the correct output

8. Python module for pow() is math and load() is pickle

   ½ mark each for the correct module

9. The protocol used for uploading and downloading the files are FTP (File Transfer Protocol)

   1 mark for naming the correct protocol

10. Cyber Stalking is a type of cyber threat / cyber activity in which a person keeps track or harass another person by misusing the internet.

    1 mark for mentioning the correct type of cyber threat

11. In SQL, order by is the clause and desc is the keyword used to display the tuples in descending order of an attribute.

    ½ mark for mentioning the correct clause
    ½ mark for the keyword to display it in descending order

12. In SQL, LIKE operator is used for pattern matching.

    1 mark for the correct operator

13. SUM / COUNT / AVERAGE / MAX / MIN

1 mark for writing any one multiple row function used in SQL

14. (b) ALTER and (d) DROP

½ mark for choosing each correct option for DDL

15. Twisted Pair cable is the transmission media consists of two insulated copper wires that are twisted together in helical form.

1 mark for writing twisted pair

16. A list is mutable whereas a tuple is immutable.

A list has a variable size while a tuple has a fixed size.

1 mark for writing any one correct difference between List and Tuple

17. nuf si nohtyP htiw gnimmargorP

1 mark for writing the correct output

18. SHOW DATABASES;

1 mark for writing the correct SQL statement

19. Advanced Research Project Agency NETwork.

1 mark for writing the full form of ARPANET

20. A table can have only one Primary key whereas a table can have multiple Unique key constraints.

Primary key will not accept NULL values whereas Unique key constraint can accept NULL values.

1 mark for any correct difference

21. Bandwidth is the maximum amount of data transmitted over the network or Internet in a given amount of time. Bandwidth is measured in bits per second (bps).

½ mark for defining bandwidth and ½ mark for the correct unit

SECTION – II

22. (a) T_ID is the attribute which is best suitable to be declared as primary key as it maintains uniqueness in the table.

1 mark for identifying the best suitable primary key

(b) Degree = 5 and cardinality = 6

½ mark for writing correct degree
½ mark for writing correct cardinality

(c) Insert into Teacher (T_ID, Name, Dept_ID)
values('106', 'Sunita', '301')

½ mark for the first part of the Insert statement
½ mark for the second part of the Insert statement

(d) (iii) DELETE FROM Teacher WHERE Salary IS NULL;

1 mark for choosing the correct option (iii)

(e) USE School;

Show Tables;

½ mark for choosing the database

½ mark for the correct query to display all the tables

23.
```
import csv                                      #Line 1

def add_student(admno, name, mobile):   #To add data to the CSV file
    with open('student.csv', 'a', newline='') as fout:   #Line 2
        n=csv.writer(fout)
        n.writerow([admno, name, mobile])

def read_student():                               #to read data from CSV file
    with open('student.csv','r') as fin:
        n=csv.reader(fin)                           #Line 3
        for r in n:
            print(r)                                #Line 4

add_student(1, "Aastha", 5566776611)
add_student(2, "Vasu", 8899001122)
add_student(3, "Charvi", 1100992211)
read_student()
```

(a) csv module OR import csv

1 mark for mentioning csv

(b) append mode to open the file to keep adding more data to the CSV file or 'a' mode

1 mark for specifying the correct mode of the file

(c) reader

1 mark for filling the blank correctly.

(d) print(r) OR r

1 mark for writing r for the record

(e) Output:

['1', 'Aastha', '5566776611']

['2', 'Vasu', '8899001122']

['3', 'Charvi', '1100992211']

1 mark for the correct output

PART – B

SECTION – I

24. (a) 3+6*4**2//3 = 35

(b) True and not(False) or False = True

1 mark for each correct output of the expression

25. Trojan Horse, or Trojan is a software which comes as an attachment to the email and looks like legitimate but once downloaded takes control of the computer. It is designed to damage, disrupt, steal or some other harmful action on your data or network.

Spam: It is also referred to as junk email, and is unsolicited messages sent in bulk by email for the purpose of advertising.

1 mark for defining each term

OR

HTML stands for Hypertext Markup Language whereas XML stands for Extensible Markup Language.

HTML has predefined tags whereas XML tags are not predefined.

HTML focus on the presentation of data whereas XML focuses on transfer of data.

1 mark for each correct difference

26. (a) SMTP: Simple Mail Transfer Protocol

(b) PAN: Personalised Area Network

(c) HTTPS: HyperText Transfer Protocol Secure

(d) POP: Post Office Protocol

½ mark for each correct full form

27. A variable defined inside a function cannot be accessed outside it. Every variable has a well-defined accessibility. The part of the program where a variable is accessible (or used) can be defined as the scope of the variable.

The two different types of variables scopes in functions are: Local scope and Global scope.

1 mark for writing the meaning of scope
½ mark for each correct type of variable scope

OR

Built-in functions are the ready-made functions in Python that are frequently used in programs. For example, input(), int(), print() are the built-in functions. The set of instructions for these built-in functions are already defined in the python interpreter.

A function is a group of statements / instructions whereas a module is a group of functions. For complex program, it may not be feasible to write the code in a single file. Therefore, the program is divided into different parts under different levels, called modules. A module is created as a python (.py) file containing a set of function definitions. To use a module, we need to import it.

For example, import ceil, floor from math

1 mark for defining built-in functions
1 mark for writing the correct difference between built-in and module

28. Corrected Code:

```
A=10                             #Error 1 - Assignment error
B=int(input('Value of B:'))  #Error 2 & 3 int() missing
if B>=A:    #Error 4 - : missing
    print(B-A)
else:           #Error 5 Indentation error
    print(A-B)
```

½ mark for mentioning and correcting each error

29. (b) 3#4#5#

Maximum value for x = 4

1 mark for choosing the correct output (b)
1 mark for writing the correct maximum value for x

30. **Primary key:** It uniquely identifies each record in a table. Primary key column contains unique values and cannot contain null values. A table can have only one primary key.

Example: Let us take the table Teacher given below:

Table: Teacher				
T_ID	**Name**	**Dept_ID**	**Salary**	**Gender**
100	Satish	041	70000	M
101	Jyotika	041	55000	F
102	Prabhjot	301	53000	F
103	Sudhanshu	042	85000	M
104	Sandeep	301	78000	M
105	Mohan	041	65000	M

In this table, T_ID maintains uniqueness and no teachers are going to have same ID. Therefore, T_ID can be taken as a primary key.

1 mark for any correct definition of primary key
1 mark for any suitable example

31. **Rowcount()** method is used to return the number of rows that are affected with the SQL statement.

For example:

import mysql.connector

mydb=mysql.connector.connect(host="localhost", user="root", passwd="root", database="School")

```
mycur=mydb.cursor()
s="SELECT * FROM Teacher"
mycur.execute(s)
print(mycur.rowcount," total records in the table")
```

1 mark for writing the correct use of rowcount() method
1 mark for suitable example

32. **DDL (Data Definition Language)** commands are used to create, manipulate and modify the structure of the table/ database.

DDL commands are Create table, Drop table, Alter table, Rename table

1 mark for writing the use of DDL commands
½ mark for each correct DDL command

33. Output:

1@5.0@5@50@

½ mark for any two correct numbers
½ mark for displaying second value as a decimal value
½ mark for displaying @ after every number

SECTION – II

34.
```
def Change_L(List1, size):
    for j in range(size):
        if List1[j] % 5 == 0:
            List1[j] = List1[j] // 5
        elif List1[j] % 3 == 0:
            List1[j] = List1[j] // 3
        elif List1[j] % 2 == 0:
            List1[j] = List1[j] // 2
        else:
            pass
    print(List1)
```

½ mark for using the loop to iterate over the elements
1 mark for checking the divisibility in the same sequence
1 mark for using the appropriate assignment statements
½ mark for displaying the final list after update

35.
```
def RevText():
    with open('input.txt', 'r') as a:
        while True:
            try:
                b = a.read()
                for i in b.split(' '):
                    if i[0].lower() == 'p':
                        print(i[::-1],end=' ')
                    else:
                        print(i,end=' ')
            except:
                break
```

½ mark for opening the file in correct mode
½ mark for reading the text file
½ mark for iterating over the words using split method
½ mark for checking the first character of each word
½ mark for displaying the word in reverse order
½ mark for displaying the word in proper order if not starts with P

36. (a)

Dept	SUM(Salary)
Mathematics	190000
Physics	85000
English	131000

(b)

Gender	COUNT(*)
F	2
M	4

(c)

Name	Dept	Salary
Sudhanshu	Physics	85000
Satish	Mathematics	70000
Sandeep	English	78000
Mohan	Mathematics	65000

1 mark for each correct output

37.
```
def Push(S, Value):
    S.append(Value)
    print(S)
```

1 mark for writing the def with argument
1 mark for adding the value at the end of the list passed as an argument
1 mark for displaying the list

OR

```
def POP(S):
    if len(S) == 0:
        print('No element')
    else:
        S.pop()
        print(S)
```

½ mark for writing the def with argument
1 mark for checking the length of the list and displaying message
1 mark for deleting the last element from the list
½ mark for displaying the list after delete operation

SECTION – III

38. STAR Topology

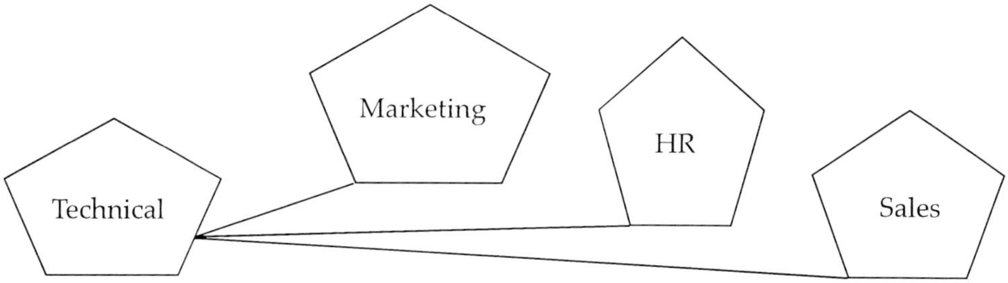

½ mark for drawing the layout
½ mark for writing the type of layout/ topology

(a) Technical is the most suitable building /department to place the server as it is having maximum number of computers in it.

½ mark for Technical department
½ mark for any correct reason

(b) Hub / Switch is to be placed/ installed in each of these departments to efficiently connect all the computers within these departments.

1 mark for mentioning any device hub/ swtich

(c) Repeater will be placed between Technical and HR department as the distance between the departments is more than 70 m.

½ mark for the correct placement
½ mark for the valid justification

(d) MAN is appropriate to link its sale counter situated in various parts of the same city. MAN is suitable to connect within same city.

½ mark for mentioning the appropriate type of network
½ mark for any valid justification

39. (a) SELECT * FROM Teacher
WHERE Dept="English";

½ mark for writing 1st part of the query
½ mark for writing 2nd part of the query

(b) SELECT Name FROM Teacher
WHERE Dept="Mathematics" AND Gender="M";

½ mark for writing 1st part of the query
½ mark for writing 2nd part of the query

(c) SELECT DEPT_ID, COUNT(*) FROM Teacher
GROUP BY DEPT_ID;

½ mark for writing 1st part of the query
½ mark for writing 2nd part of the query

(d) UPDATE Teacher SET Salary=Salary+Salary*10/100
WHERE DEPT_ID='041'

½ mark for writing 1st part of the query
½ mark for writing 2nd part of the query

(e) SELECT Name, Dept, Salary Gender FROM Teacher, Department
WHERE Teacher.DEPT_ID=Department.DEPT_ID and Gender="M";

½ mark for writing 1st part of the query
½ mark for writing 2nd part of the query

40. (a)

```
import pickle


def CreateEmp():
    with open('Emp.dat', 'ab') as a:
        en = input("Enter Employee Number:")
        em = input('Enter Name:')
        de = input('Enter Department:')
        sa = input('Enter Salary:')
        rec = [en, em, de, sa]
        pickle.dump(rec, a)
```

½ mark for importing pickle module
½ mark for opening the file in correct mode
½ mark for reading the contents for the record
1 mark for writing the contents using dump method

(b)

```
import pickle

def Ctr_Rec(Department):
    with open('Emp.dat', 'rb') as a:
        c = 0
        while True:
            try:
                Rec = pickle.load(a)
                if Department == Rec[2]:
                    c += 1
            except:
                break
        return 'No of people in department', c
```

½ mark for import pickle
½ mark for reading the file in correct mode
½ mark for reading the record from the data file
½ mark for checking the department as per the argument
½ mark for incrementing the counter and returning the counter value

OR

```
import pickle
def Check_Balance():
    c = 0
    with open('Bank.dat', 'rb') as a:
        while True:
            try:
                Rec = pickle.load(a)
                if Rec[3] < 2000:
                    print(Rec)
                    c += 1
            except:
                break
        print("Total number of customers with balance less than 2000: ",c)
```

½ mark for pickle module
1 mark for opening the file in correct mode
1 mark for reading the record from the data file
1 mark for checking the salary less than 2000
½ mark for incrementing the counter variable
1 mark for the final display statement

Solved Sample Paper – 2 (Theory)

M.M.: 70 **Time: 3 hrs**

General Instructions

1. This question paper contains two parts A and B. Each part is compulsory.
2. Both Part A and Part B have choices.
3. Part-A has 2 sections:
   a. Section – I is short answer questions, to be answered in one word or one line.
   b. Section – II has two case studies questions. Each case study has 4 case-based subparts. An examinee is to attempt any 4 out of the 5 subparts.
4. Part - B is Descriptive Paper.
5. Part- B has three sections
   a. Section-I is short answer questions of 2 marks each in which two question have internal options.
   b. Section-II is long answer questions of 3 marks each in which two questions have internal options.
   c. Section-III is very long answer questions of 5 marks each in which one question has internal option.
6. All programming questions are to be answered using Python Language only.

PART – A

SECTION – I

Attempt any 15 questions from question numbers 1 to 21. Each question carries 1 mark. **(1 × 15 = 15 marks)**

1. Write the following operators according to their precedence of operations: 1

   +, *, / /, **

2. Given below the following list: 1

   List1=[{'Maths':84},{'Science':47},{'English':78}]

   print(List1[0].keys(), List1[2].values())

3. Differentiate among the following: 1

   (a) a = open('story.txt', 'r')

   (b) a = open('story.txt', 'w')

4. Define comment. How to write a comment in Python? 1

5. Write any two Data Types in Python. 1

6. Write a python statement to declare a list of tuples containing the following (301, English), (054, Accounts). 1

7. What is the use of membership operators? Also, name the membership operators. 1

8. Name the function/ method used to perform the following: 1

   (a) Check if a string contains only lowercase letters.

   (b) Gives the total number of elements of the list.

9. Which protocol is used to connect to the internet? 1

10. Out of the following, which all comes under cybercrime? 1

    (a) Getting someone's social networking password without his consent and posting on his behalf.

    (b) Secretly taken someone's project and then sending it as your own.

    (c) Looking for some information over internet.

    (d) Stealing mouse from your friend house.

11. Write the output produced by the following SQL statements: 1

    (a) SELECT POW(3, 3);

    (b) SELECT LEFT("Computer Science", 4);

12. Name the range matching operator which includes both the lower and upper limits. 1

13. Name the SQL functions for the following operations: 1

    (a) To convert the string into lowercase.

    (b) To return the number of characters in the specified string.

14. Write the DDL statement to add a primary key to the column BOOKID in the existing table Books. 1

15. Define topology. Name any two topologies. 1

16. Write a python statement to perform the following operations: 1

    (a) To assign "Mathematics" to a variable subject.

    (b) To display "mat" from the subject.

17. Define Dictionary in Python with the help of an example. 1

18. Write a SQL statement to display the list of tables in the database. 1

19. Illustrate the layout for connecting 6 computers in a Star and Linear/Bus topology of networks. 1

20. Write any one difference between ALTER and UPDATE statement. 1

21. Out of the following, which is the fastes (a) wired and (b) wireless communication?
Infrared, Coaxial Cable, Ethernet Cable, Microwave, Optical Fiber 1

SECTION – II

Consists of case study questions and are compulsory to attempt. Attempt any 4 sub parts from each question. Each sub part carries 1 mark. (4 + 4 = 8 marks)

22. A bookstore is about to maintain their books' details using SQL to store the data for inventory. As a database administrator, you have decided to declare the following to create the inventory:

- Name of the database – Bookstore
- Name of the table – Books
- The attributes of Books are:

  BookID – numeric value of integer type

  AuthorID – character of size 5

  PubID – character of size 4

  Title – character of size 15

  Price – numeric value of integer type

Table: Books

BookID	AuthorID	PubID	Title	Price
100	A01	P01	Accountancy I	100
101	A02	P02	Mathematics I	180
102	A01	P01	Accountancy II	150
103	A03	P04	Psychology	125
104	A05	P04	Business Studies	NULL
105	A02	P01	Mathematics II	210

(a) Identify the most appropriate attribute as primary key. 1

(b) Write the SQL statement to create the database BookStore and also to change the current database as Bookstore. 1

(c) Write the DDL statement to create the structure of the table Books. Primary key and Not Null constraints have to be applied to the appropriate columns.
[*Note:* Attribute description is given above the table.] 1

(d) Write the SQL statement to display the structure of the table. 1

(e) Write SQL statement to insert a record in the BOOKS table with following information: 1
BookID =210, AuthorID ="A10", PubID="P03", Title="Computer Science I"

23. Abhimanyu has created a csv file "bank.csv" which contains the AccNo, Name and Balance for all the customers. He has written the following code to read all the details from "bank.csv" file and display the details of the selected customers. As a programmer, help him to fill up the blanks so as to successfully execute the code.

The data added to the file bank.csv is:

10000	Aastha	20000
10001	Charvi	13000
10002	Diya	15000

```
import ____________                         #Line 1

def disp():
    with open("__________","r") as fin:    #Line 2
        file=csv.reader(fin)
        ctr=_____                           #Line 3 to initialise counter
        for rec in file:
            ctr+=1
            if _____(rec[2])>=15000:        #Line 4
                print(rec)
        print("Total number of records in bank.csv: ",ctr)

disp()
```

(a) Name the module to be imported to fill up the blank in Line 1. 1

(b) Fill up the blank for Line 2. 1

(c) Fill up the blank for Line 3 to initialise the counter variable to zero. 1

(d) Fill up the blank in Line 4 with appropriate function/method to convert text field to numeric field. 1

(e) Write the output of the program while executing the code. 1

PART - B

SECTION – I

Each question carries 2 marks **(2 × 10 = 20)**

24. Differentiate between Syntax Error and Logical Error with the help of an example. 2

25. Define cookies. What kind of data gets stored in cookies and how is it useful? 2

OR

Differentiate between packet switching and circuit switching with the help of an example.

26. Expand the following terms: 2

(a) DNS (b) TCP/IP (c) URL (d) TDMA

27. Differentiate between Argument and Parameter with the help of an example. 2

OR

What is default parameter? Explain it with the help of an example.

28. Rewrite the following code in Python after removing all the syntax error(s). Underline each correction done in the code. 2

```
def Sum_Range(N):
      S=0
      for x in range(1, N+1):
            S+=x
      return S
print(Sum_Range(4))
print(Sum_Range(5))
```

29. What are the possible outcome(s) executed from the following code? Also, specify the maximum and minimum values that can be assigned to the variable R. 2

```
import random
Str="quarantine"
R=random.randint(0,3)

X=len(Str)
for i in range(R+1):
      print(Str[i]+"$"+Str[i+1]+"$")
```

(a) qa (b) q$u (c) q$u$ (d) u$ 2

30. Write one similarity and one difference between Primary key and Unique constraint. 2

31. Write the steps to select data from any database using Python program. 2

Steps to be followed to select the data from any of the database using Python program are:

32. Define Cardinality Product. Create the cartesian product on the given two tables. Also, write the degree and cardinality after cartesian product on the given tables: 2

Table: Books		
BID	**Title**	**Price**
100	Computer Science XI	230
201	Computer Science XII	245

Table: Author	
AID	**Name**
A01	Mukesh
A02	Kavita

33. Find and write the output of the following Python code: 2

```
for City in ['Delhi','Mumbai','Calcutta','Madras']:
    print(City)
    if City[0]=='M':
        break
    else:
        print('Finished')
print("Done")
```

SECTION – II

Each question carries 3 marks **(3 × 4 = 12)**

34. Write a user defined function Dispay() in Python which takes a list as an argument and display the elements of the list in such a manner that if it consists of a digit then it will display it twice otherwise the element will be displayed terminated by a '$' character. 3

For example, if the content of the list passed to the Display(List1) function is as follows:

```
L = ['34', 'Annu', 'Kavita', '67', 'Balwinder']
Then the output will be:
3434
Annu$
Kavita$
6767
Balwinder$
```

35. Write a function DispI() in Python to read the content from a text file "Story.txt" line by line and display those lines which starts with the character 'I'. 3

36. Write output for the following SQL queries (a) to (c) based on the relations DEPT and EMPLOYEE given below: 3

Table: DEPT

DCODE	DEPARTMENT	CITY
D01	MEDIA	MUMBAI
D02	MARKETING	DELHI
D03	FINANCE	DELHI
D04	HUMAN RESOURCE	MUMBAI

Table: Employee

WID	NAME	DOJ	GENDER	DCODE
101	Kavita	2019-09-02	F	D01
102	Amita	2018-01-10	F	D04
103	Sandeep	2019-04-28	M	D02
104	Abhimanyu	2018-05-20	M	D01
105	Balwinder	2017-07-20	F	D02
106	Annu	2017-12-21	F	D03
107	Pratibha	2019-05-19	F	D01

(a) SELECT MAX(DOJ), MIN(DOJ) FROM Employee;

(b) SELECT DISTINCT CITY FROM Dept;

(c) SELECT NAME, GENDER, DEPARTMENT
FROM Employee E, DEPT D
WHERE E.DCODE=D.DCODE;

37. Write a function PUSH(Books) in Python for performing Push operations on a List of Books. Assuming the parameter Books as a list for implementing the stack which consists of elements containing dictionary of key-value pairs for Bno, Bname and Price. Display the contents of the Books. 3

OR

Write a function POP(Books) in Python for performing Pop operations on a Stack. Assuming the parameter Books as a list for implementing the stack which consists of elements containing dictionary of key-value pairs for bno, bname and price. Also, display an appropriate error message for empty list.

SECTION – III

Each question carries 5 marks **(5 × 3 = 15)**

38. ACM Edu. Ltd is an educational institute. It is planning to setup its India campus at Delhi with its head office at Jammu. The Delhi campus has 4 buildings – ADMIN, BUISNESS, MARKETING, TECHNICAL. 5

You are a network expert who has to suggest the best network related solutions for their problems raised in (a) to (e), keeping in mind the distances between the buildings and other given parameters.

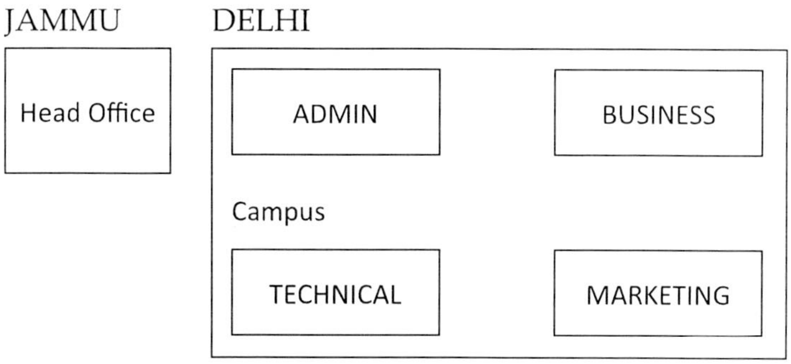

Shortest distances between various buildings:

ADMIN to TECHNICAL	65 km
TECHNICAL to BUSINESS	100 km
TECHNICAL to MARKETING	50 km
MARKETING to ADMIN	110 km
MARKETING to BUSINESS	80 km
BUSINESS to TECHNICAL	120 km
JAMMU HEAD OFFICE to DELHI	589 km

Number of computers installed at various buildings are as follows:

ADMIN	100
BUSINESS	15
TECHNICAL	120
MARKETING	20
JAMMU HEAD OFFICE	25

(a) Suggest the most suitable place to house the server in Delhi Campus (out of the 4 buildings), to get the best connectivity for maximum number of computers. Justify your answer.

(b) Suggest and draw the cable layout to efficiently connect various buildings within Delhi campus for connecting the computers.

(c) Which device /software will you suggest to be installed to protect and control the internet threats to the network in the campus?

(d) Which device will you suggest to connect computers within each department/ building?

(e) What is repeater? Suggest the placement of a repeater in the network.

39. Write the SQL commands for the following queries (a) to (e) based on the relations DEPT and WORKER tables. 5

Table: DEPT

DCODE	DEPARTMENT	CITY
D01	MEDIA	MUMBAI
D02	MARKETING	DELHI
D03	FINANCE	DELHI
D04	HUMAN RESOURCE	MUMBAI

Table: WORKER

WID	NAME	DOJ	GENDER	DCODE
101	Kavita	2019-09-02	F	D01
102	Amita	2018-01-10	F	D04
103	Sandeep	2019-04-28	M	D02
104	Abhimanyu	2018-05-20	M	D01
105	Balwinder	2017-07-20	F	D02
106	Annu	2017-12-21	F	D03
107	Pratibha	2019-05-19	F	D01

(a) To display the WID, Name, Gender from table Worker in descending order of WID.

(b) To display the name of female workers from the Workers table.

(c) To display the WID and Name of those workers from workers table who joined in the year 2017.

(d) To count and display the total number of workers in each department.

(e) To display Name, Gender, Department from tables DEPT and WORKER.

40. A binary file "Member.dat" has the following structure [MNO, MNAME, MOBILE]. 5

(a) Write a user defined function CREATEMEM() in Python to accept the values for the member record and add it to the pickled file "Member.dat".

(b) Write a user defined function DISPLAY() in Python which will read all the records from the pickled file "Member.dat" and display.

OR

A binary file "Stud.dat" has structure (Rno, Name, Aggregate). Write a function Search(Agg) in Python which takes Agg as parameter that would read contents of the pickled file "Stud.dat", display all those students from "Stud.dat" who scored more than Agg. Also, count and return the number of students who scored more than Agg from "Stud.dat".

Solved Sample Paper – 2 (Theory) - Answers

PART – A

SECTION – I

1. **, *, //, +

½ mark for any two correct operator precedence

2. dict_keys(['Maths']) dict_values([78])

½ mark each for the correct dict_keys() and dict_values()

3. Statement (a) opens the file in read mode whereas statement (b) opens the file in write mode.

1 mark for the correct difference

4. Comment in Python is a remark which is not checked for any errors by the interpreter. Hash (#) symbol is used to write comments in Python.

1 mark for defining comment
1 mark for mentioning any correct way of declaring comments in Python

5. Numbers (Integer/Boolean/ Float) / Sequence(Strings/ Lists/ Tuples)/ Sets/ None/ Mappings (Dictionary)

½ mark for each correct data type in python

6. List1=[('301', 'English'), ('054', 'Accounts')]

1 mark for writing correct statement

7. Membership operators are used to check if a value is a member of the given sequence or not. Membership operators are:
   (a) in
   (b) not in

½ mark for the use of membership operators
½ mark for writing both the membership operators

8. (a) islower()
   (b) len()

½ mark each for the correct function/ method

9. TCP/IP is used to connect the computers to communicate using the internet.

1 mark naming the correct protocol

10. (a) Getting someone's social networking password without his consent and posting on his behalf.
    (b) Secretly taken someone's project and then sending it as your own.

1 mark for choosing both the correct options

11. (a) 27

(b) Comp

½ mark for each correct output

12. BETWEEN is the range matching operator which includes both the lower and upper limits.

1 mark for the correct operator

13. (a) Lower(str)

(b) Mid(str, x, y) / substring(str, x, y)

½ mark for each correct function name

14. ALTER TABLE Books ADD Primary Key(BOOKID);

½ mark for ALTER TABLE BOOKS and
½ mark for ADD Primary Key(BookID)

15. Topology is the arrangement of computers or devices in a network which are connected to each other. Topologies – Star / Bus (Linear)/ Ring/ Mesh

½ mark for defining topology
½ mark for naming any two topology

16. (a) Subject="Mathematics"

(b) print(Left(Subject,3))

½ mark for each correct python statement

17. Dictionary is a mapping between a set of keys and set of values. The key-value pair is called an item. A key is separated from its value using a colon (:) and consecutive items are separated by commas. Dictionary is written within curly brackets.

For example: dict={"1":"Sunday", "2":"Monday"}

½ mark for defining dictionary and ½ mark for example

18. SHOW Tables;

1 mark for the correct SQL statement

19. Illustrate the layout for connecting 6 computers in a Star topology of networks.

STAR Topology for connecting 6 computers

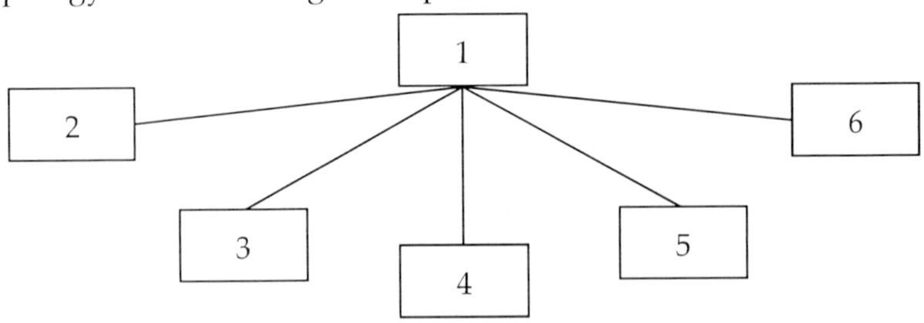

1 mark for drawing 6 computers in Star topology

20. ALTER is DDL command whereas UPDATE is a DML command.

ALTER table can make changes in the structure of the table whereas UPDATE can make changes in the records of the table.

1 mark for any correct difference

21. Wired: Optical Fibre

Wireless: Infrared OR Microwave

½ mark for each correct answer

SECTION – II

22. (a) BookID is the primary key

1 mark for choosing the correct primary key

(b) CREATE DATABASE BOOKSTORE;

USE BOOKSTORE;

½ mark for the first statement

½ mark for the second statement

(c) CREATE TABLE Books (BookID int Primary key,

AuthorID char(3) NOT NULL, PubID char(3), Title char(20), Price int);

½ mark for the Create table statement

½ mark for the attributes with primary key and not null

(d) DESC Books;

1 mark for the correct statement

(e) INSERT INTO Books(BookID, AuthorID, PubID, Title)

VALUES(210, "A10", "P03", "Computer Science I");

½ mark for the first part of insert statement

½ mark for the second part of insert statement

23.
```
import csv

def disp():
    with open("Bank.csv","r") as fin:
        file=csv.reader(fin)
        ctr=0
        for rec in file:
            ctr+=1
            if int(rec[2])>=15000:
                print(rec)
        print("Total number of records in bank.csv: ",ctr)

disp()
```

(a) csv module / import csv

1 mark for writing the name of the module or the correct statement

(b) Bank.csv

1 mark for mentioning the correct data file

(c) 0 / ctr=0

1 mark for correct initialisation of ctr

(d) int/ float

1 mark for using any of the numeric method int or float

(e) Output:

['10000', 'Aastha', '20000']

['10002', 'Diya', '15000']

Total number of records in bank.csv: 3

½ mark for displaying both the records

½ mark for displaying the total number of records in bank.csv:3

PART – B

SECTION – I

24. Syntax Error is the error which is encountered by the interpreter when Python rules are not followed while writing the code.

For example: colon missing at the end of if statement is a syntax error.

Logical Error is the type of error which is difficult to debug. It occurs when the program runs but gives an incorrect output. This error is caused due to mistake in the program's logic. For example: Using addition symbol instead of multiply will give wrong output.

½ mark each for defining syntax error and logical error

½ mark each for example of syntax error and logical error

25. Cookies are text files with small pieces of data that is used to identify the user. It can store a wide range of information, including personal details like name, email, mobile, etc.

Cookies are used by the websites to store browsing information of the user.

1 mark for correct definition of cookies

½ mark for mentioning the kind of data stored in cookies

½ mark for mentioning its usage

OR

Packet switching is a technique in which the message or information is broken down into packets of fixed length whereas Circuit switching is a technique in which the circuit (i.e. dedicated path) has to be established before data transfer.

SMS is an example of packet switching. If a user sends a long message then it gets transferred in smaller data packets and are charged as per number of packets.

Telephone network system is one of the examples of circuit switching.

1 mark for any correct difference
½ mark each for example

26. (a) **DNS:** Domain Name Server
    (b) **TCP/IP:** Transmission Control Protocol / Internet Protocol
    (c) **URL:** Uniform Resource Locator
    (d) **TDMA:** Time Division Multiple Access

½ mark for each correct full form

27. An argument is a value passed to the function during the function call statement which is received in corresponding parameter defined in function header. A parameter is defined in the function header and it accepts the value from the function call statement.

For example:

```
def sum(a, b):
    return a + b
c=sum(3, 5)
```

In the above example, 3 and 5 are arguments as it is used in the function call statement whereas a and b are parameters as it is used in the function definition.

½ mark each for defining argument and parameter
½ mark each for the any correct example of argument and parameter

OR

A default value is a value that is assigned to the parameter and is used when the function call statement does not provide any argument for the respective parameter.

For example:

```
def calc(a, b=2):
    return a**b
calc(2,4) #function call 1
calc(3) #function call 2
```

In the above example, function call 1 statement is invoked with two arguments whereas function call 2 statement has one argument so in place of second argument default value of b=2 will be used.

1 mark for any correct definition of default parameter
1 mark for any correct example of default parameter

28. def Sum_Range(N) #Error 1 – Colon missing

```
def Sum_Range(N)                #Error 1 – Colon missing
    S=0
    for x in Range(1, N+1):     #Error 2 – Range is misspelled
        S+=x
    RETURN S                    #Error 3 – RETURN is misspelled
print(Sum_Range(4))
print(Sum_Range(5, 7))          #Error 4 – two arguments used instead of one
```

Corrected Code:

```
def Sum_Range(N):
    S=0
    for x in range(1, N+1):
        S+=x
    return S
print(Sum_Range(4))
print(Sum_Range(5))
```

½ mark for correcting each error

29. Correct option of output: (c) qu

Maximum value of R = 3

Minimum value of R = 0

1 mark for choosing the correct output
½ mark each for the correct maximum and minimum value of R

30. Primary key and Unique constraint maintains uniqueness in the table.

There can be only one primary key in a table whereas more than one attribute can be set as Unique constraint.

Primary key doesn't allow Null values whereas Unique allows to enter Null values.

1 mark for any correct similarity
1 mark for any correct difference

31. Steps to be followed to select the data from any of the database using Python program are:

1) Establish a connection to the database using connect() method.
2) Create a cursor object from the connection object using connection.cursor() method.
3) Execute SQL statement to get the data from one or more tables using cursor.execute() method.
4) Fetch rows using cursor.fetchone() and cursor.fetchall() methods.

5) Finally release the cursor and connections objects using the cursor.close() and connection.close() methods.

½ mark for each correct step and Ignore close() method

32. Cardinality Product gives the cross product of two tables in which it combines tuples from two relations. It results in all pairs of rows from the two input relations, regardless of whether or not they have the common attributes or same values. The degree of the resulting table is calculated as sum of the degree of underlying tables and cardinality is calculated as the product of the cardinality of both the tables.

Books x Author				
BID	**Title**	**Price**	**AID**	**Name**
100	Computer Science XI	230	A01	Mukesh
100	Computer Science XI	230	A02	Kavita
201	Computer Science XII	245	A01	Mukesh
201	Computer Science XII	245	A02	Kavita

Degree = 5

Cardinality = 4

½ mark for defining cartesian product
½ mark for creating the cartesian product out of the given tables
½ mark each for writing the correct degree and cardinality of the final table

33. Output:

Delhi

Finished

Mumbai

Done

½ mark for each correct line of output

SECTION – II

34.
```
def Display(List1):
    for i in List1:
        if i.isdigit():
            print(i*2)
        else:
            print(i+'$')

L = ['34', 'Annu', 'Kavita', '67', 'Balwinder']
Display(L)
```

½ mark for the list argument to the function
½ mark using the for loop to iterate over the list elements
1 mark for checking list elements containing digits
½ mark for printing the duplicate values for the digits
½ mark for displaying $ at the end of the list element if it is not a digit

35.
```
def displ():
    with open('story.txt','r')as fin:
        while True:
            a=fin.readline()
            if not a:
                break
            if a[0].upper()=='I':
                print(a)

displ()
```

½ mark for opening the file in the correct mode
½ mark for while loop
½ mark for reading a line
½ exiting the loop if reaching end of file
½ mark for checking the first character of line as I
½ mark for the display of the line starting with I

36. (a)

MAX(DOJ)	MIN(DOJ)
2019-09-02	2017-07-20

1 mark for the correct output

(b)

CITY
MUMBAI
DELHI

1 mark for the correct output

(c)

NAME	GENDER	DEPARTMENT
Kavita	F	MEDIA
Amita	F	HUMAN RESOURCE
Sandeep	M	MARKETING
Abhimanyu	M	MEDIA
Balwinder	F	MARKETING
Annu	F	FINANCE
Pratibha	F	MEDIA

1 mark for the correct output

37.
```
def PUSH(Books):
    bn=input("Enter book no")
    na=input("Enter book name")
    p=float(input("Enter price"))
    rec={}
    rec={'bno':bn,'bname':na,'price':p}
    Books.append(rec)
    print(Books)

Books=[{'bno':'041','bname':'NCERT Maths 10','price':200}]
PUSH(Books)
```

1 mark for reading the contents for the record
½ mark for making it as a dictionary
1 mark for adding the record to the end of the list
½ mark for displaying the list of dictionaries as elements of list

OR

```
def POP(Books):
    if len(Books)==0:
        print("Underflow")
    else:
        print(Books.pop()," deleted successfully")

Books=[{'bno':'041','bname':'NCERT Maths 10','price':200}]
POP(Books)
```

1 mark for checking the empty list and ½ mark displaying an appropriate message
1 mark for deleting the element
½ mark for displaying the deleted element

SECTION – III

38. (a) The most suitable place to house the server in Delhi Campus (out of the 4 buildings), to get the best connectivity for maximum number of computers is TECHNICAL building because of maximum number of computers in that building.

½ mark for TECHNICAL building
½ mark for mentioning the reason

(b) Topology – STAR

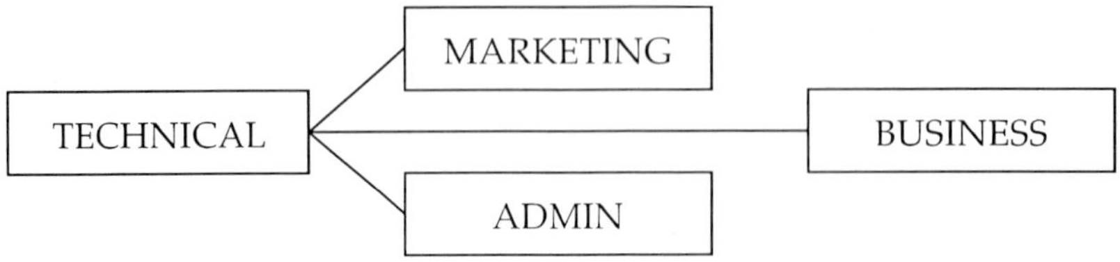

½ mark for naming the topology
½ mark for drawing the layout

(c) Firewall to be installed to protect and control the internet threats to the network in the campus.

1 mark for the correct answer

(d) Hub / Switch is to connect computers within each department/ building.

1 mark for the correct answer.

(e) A repeater is a networking device which is used to amplify the incoming signal and then transmit the boosted signal. The repeater can be used between TECHNICAL and BUSINESS buildings as the distance between these buildings is more than 70km.

½ mark for any correct definition of repeater
½ mark for the placement of repeater

39. (a) SELECT WID, Name, Gender FROM Worker
ORDER BY WID desc;

½ mark for the first part of the SQL statement
½ mark for the second part of the SQL statement

(b) SELECT Name FROM Worker
WHERE Gender = 'F';

½ mark for the first part of the SQL statement
½ mark for the second part of the SQL statement

(c) SELECT WID, Name FROM Worker
WHERE YEAR(DOJ) = 2017;

½ mark for the first part of the SQL statement
½ mark for the second part of the SQL statement

(d) SELECTT COUNT(DCODE), DCODE FROM Worker
GROUP BY DCODE;

OR

SELECT Department, COUNT(W.Dcode) FROM WORKER W, DEPT D WHERE W.Dcode=D.Dcode GROUP BY Department;

½ mark for the first part of the SQL statement
½ mark for the second part of the SQL statement

(e) SELECT Name, Gender, Department FROM DEPT, WORKER
WHERE DEPT.DCODE=WORKER.DCODE;

½ mark for the first part of the SQL statement
½ mark for the second part of the SQL statement

40.
```
import pickle

def CREATEMEM():
    with open("Member.dat","ab")as fout:
        mn=input("Enter Member number")
        nm=input("Enter Member name")
        mb=input("Enter Mobile")
        R=[mn, nm, mb]
        pickle.dump(R,fout)

def DISPLAY():
    with open('Member.dat','rb') as fin:
        while True:
            try:
                R=pickle.load(fin)
                print(R)
            except:
                break

CREATEMEM()
DISPLAY()
```

½ mark for import pickler
½ mark for opening the file in correct mode
1 mark for reading the contents
½ mark for writing into the data file
½ mark for opening the file in correct mode
½ mark for while loop
½ mark for reading each record from the data file
½ mark for displaying information
½ mark for try and except block

OR

```
import pickle

def Search(Agg):
    with open('Stud.dat','rb') as fin:
```

```
        ctr=0
        while True:
            try:
                a=pickle.load(fin)
                if a[2]>=Agg:
                    print(a)
                    ctr+=1
            except:
                break
        return ctr

x=float(input("Enter the aggregate above which records are to be searched"))
r=Search(x)
print("Total no of records more than ",x," : ", r)
```

½ mark for import pickle
½ mark for opening the file in correct mode
½ mark for while loop
½ mark for try-except block
½ mark for initialising the counter variable
½ mark for reading the record from the data file
½ mark for checking the condition to display selected records
½ mark for displaying the selected record using the print statement
½ mark for incrementing the counter
½ mark for returning the counter

Solved Sample Paper – 3 (Theory)

M.M.: 70 **Time: 3 hrs**

General Instructions

1. This question paper contains two parts A and B. Each part is compulsory.
2. Both Part A and Part B have choices.
3. Part-A has 2 sections:
   a. Section – I is short answer questions, to be answered in one word or one line.
   b. Section – II has two case studies questions. Each case study has 4 case-based subparts. An examinee is to attempt any 4 out of the 5 subparts.
4. Part - B is Descriptive Paper.
5. Part- B has three sections
   a. Section-I is short answer questions of 2 marks each in which two question have internal options.
   b. Section-II is long answer questions of 3 marks each in which two questions have internal options.
   c. Section-III is very long answer questions of 5 marks each in which one question has internal option.
6. All programming questions are to be answered using Python Language only.

PART – A

SECTION – I

Attempt any 15 questions from question numbers 1 to 21. Each question carries 1 mark. **(1 × 15 = 15 marks)**

1. Out of the following, find those identifiers, which cannot be used for naming variable or function in a Python program: 1

(a) Qty*Price (b) class (c) If (d) 4no

(e) Total (f) Subject3 (g) _Amt (h) First name

2. Write a statement in Python to assign strings 'Computer Science', 'Mathematics', 'English' to variables 'Sub1', 'Sub', 'Sub' respectively. 1

3. Write a statement in Python to perform the following operations: 1

(a) To open a text file "Story.txt" in read mode.

(b) To open a text file "Story.txt" in append mode.

4. Write the output for the following code: 1

```
Examination = "CBSE"
for i in Examination:
   print(i, end='$')
```

5. Define implicit conversion with an example. 1

6. Give the output of the following Python statement. 1

```
when n1=2, n2=3 and n3=4:
n1 ** = n2 + n3
print(n1)
```

7. What is the use of identity operators? Also, name the identity operators. 1

8. Name the Python Library modules which need to be imported to invoke the following functions: 1

   (a) dump()

   (b) remove()

9. Which protocol helps us to browse through Web pages using Internet browsers? Name any one Internet browser. 1

10. Mr. Sanjay is an IT expert. He recently used his skills to access the Admin password for the network server of ABC Pvt. Ltd. and provided the confidential data of the organisation to its CEO, informing him about the vulnerability of their network security. Out of the following (a) to (d) options, which one most appropriately defines Mr. Sanjay. 1

    Justify your answer.

    (a) Operator (b) Hacker

    (c) Network Administrator (d) Cracker

11. Define Domain in SQL. Also, give a suitable example. 1

12. Write the list matching operator in SQL. 1

13. Name any two Date functions in SQL. 1

14. What is the use of Foreign key in SQL? 1

15. Define Computer Virus. 1

16. Give one example each for Runtime Error and Syntax Error. 1

17. Name any two iteration statements in Python. 1

18. Write the DDL statement to set the foreign key Acode in the table Transaction for the reference table Account. 1

19. Write any one difference between Website and Web page. 1

20. Write any one difference between DELETE and DROP statement. 1

21. Give one suitable example of URL and domain name each. 1

SECTION – II

Consists of case study questions and are compulsory to attempt. Attempt any 4 sub parts from each question. Each sub part carries 1 mark. (4 + 4 = 8 marks)

22. A video store is about to maintain their video details using SQL to store the data for inventory. As a database administrator, you have decided to declare the following to create the inventory:

- Name of the database – VideoStore
- Name of the table – Video
- The attributes of Video are:

  VCode – character of size 3

  Title – character of size 30 (Not Null constraint)

  Type – character of size 15

  Price – numeric value of type integer

  Qty – numeric value of type integer

Table: Video

VCode	Title	Type	Price	Qty
H01	Dawn of the Dead	Horror	250	3
H02	Evil Dead	Horror	120	2
F01	Interstellar	Fiction	235	4
C01	Caddyshack	Comedy	341	4
H03	The Cabin in the Woods	Horror	225	2
F02	The Invisible Ma	Fiction	346	3

(a) Identify the most appropriate attribute as primary key. 1

(b) Write the SQL statement to create the database VideoStore and also to change the current database as Bookstore. 1

(c) Write the DDL statement to create the structure of the table Video. Primary key and Not Null constraints have to be applied to the appropriate columns. 1

(d) Write the SQL statement to display the structure of the table. 1

(e) Write SQL statement to insert a record in the Video table with following information:

("C02", "Hera Pheri", "Comedy", 304, 5) 1

23. Annu wants to create a csv file "Order.csv" which contains the order details such as OrderNo, ProdID, Qty and UPrice. She has written the following code so as to add more records for ordering the products and display all the order details. As a programmer, help her to rectify the errors by filling in the blanks.

```
def Add_Rec(L):
    with open("order.csv","w",newline='') as C:
        cw=csv.writer(C)
        header=['OrderNo','Prod_ID','Qty','UPrice']
        cw.writerow(header)
        cw.writerow(L)

def Add_More(L):
    with open('order.csv','____',newline='') as C:    #Line 1
        cw=csv.writer(C)
        cw.__________(L)                              #Line 2

def Display():
    with open('order.csv','r') as C:
        cr=csv.reader(C)
        for x in _____:                               #Line 3
            print(x)

Add_Rec([1, 'P01', 29, 20])
Add_More([2, 'P02', 10, 100])
Add_More([3, 'P03', 12, 25])
Display()
```

(a) Help Annu to rectify the following error while executing the code as: NameError: name 'csv' is not defined. 1

(b) Fill in the blank for Line 1. 1

(c) Fill in the blank for Line 2. 1

(d) Fill in the blank for Line 3. 1

(e) Write the output of the program while executing the code. 1

PART – B

SECTION – I

Each question carries 2 marks **(2 × 10 = 20)**

24. Define Explicit Conversion. Name any two explicit type conversion functions in Python. 2

25. Classify each of the following Web Scripting as Client-Side Scripting and Server-Side Scripting: 2

(a) ASP (b) VB Scripting (c) JSP (d) Java Scripting

OR

Write any two differences between Bus Topology and Star Topology.

26. Write the full form of the following: 2

(a) GSM (b) GPRS (c) WLL (d) WWW

27. Define break and continue statement in Python. 2

OR

Write the purpose of range() function with the help of an example.

28. Rewrite the following code in Python after removing all syntax error(s). Underling each correction done in the code. 2

```
for City in (Delhi, Mumbai, Calcutta, Madras)
    if City[0]=='M'
        print(City)
```

29. What are the possible outcome(s) after executing the following code? Also, specify the maximum and minimum values that can be assigned to variable C. 2

```
import random
C=random.randint(0, 2)
CITY=['DELHI','JAMMU','CHANDIGARH','MUMBAI']
for I in CITY:
    for J in range(C):
        print(I, end="")
    print()
```

(a)	(c)
DELHI JAMMU CHANDIGARH MUMBAI	DELHIDELHI JAMMUJAMMU CHANDIGARHCHANDIGARH MUMBAIMUMBAI
(b)	(d)
DELHIJAMMU JAMMUCHANDIGARH CHANDIGARHMUMBAI	DELHI CHANDIGARH MUMBAI JAMMU

30. Observe the following tables Student and Dance carefully and write the name of the RDBMS operation which will be used to produce the output as shown in Participant. Also, find the degree and cardinality of the table Participant. 2

Table: STUDENT

SNO	NAME
1	Lakshya
2	Devansh
3	Abhi

Table: DANCE

Dcode	Name
101	Sanchita
102	Charvi

SNO	NAME	Dcode	Name
1	Lakshya	101	Sanchita
1	Lakshya	102	Charvi
2	Devansh	101	Sanchita
2	Devansh	102	Charvi
3	Abhi	101	Sanchita
3	Abhi	102	Charvi

31. Tanya has written the Python code to fetch the information from SQL database to display all the records of table Music from the database School. Also, she displayed the total number of records present in the table Music.

You as a database manager, help her to fill in the statements so as to execute the code successfully.

```
import mysql.connector
mydb=mysql.connector.connect(host="localhost",user="root",
                    passwd="root", database="_______") #Line 1

mycursor=mydb.cursor()
s="SELECT * FROM _________"                        #Line 2
mycursor.execute(s)
result=mycursor.____________()                     #Line 3
print(result)
print("Total number of records: ",_______________) #Line 4
```

(a) Fill in the blank for Line 1

(b) Fill in the blank for Line 2 to read all the records from Dance table.

(c) Fill in the blank for Line 3 to read all the records from the table using cursor after executing the SQL statement.

(d) Fill in the blank for Line 4 to display the total number of records fetched from the table using cursor. 2

32. Define RDBMS. Name any two popular RDBMS software. 2

33. Find and write the output of the following Python code: 2

```
Data=["A","B","C","D"]
Times=0
Alpha=""
for C in range(0,4):
    Times=Times+C
    Alpha=Alpha+Data[C]+"$"
    print(Times, Alpha)
```

SECTION – II

Each question carries 3 marks **(3 × 4 = 12)**

34. Write a function Prime(N) in Python to find and display the prime numbers between 2 to N where N is passed as an argument to the function. 3

35. Write a function Search() in Python to read the content from a text file "Places. txt" to find, count and display the words where the number of characters are more than 7. 3

For example: The contents of Places.txt is as shown below:

I love to explore different places in the world.

This is so exiting and different to get the feel of various cultures.

The program will give the following output:

different different cultures

Total number of words with length more than 7 = 3

36. Write output for the following SQL queries (a) to (c) based on the relations ACCOUNT and TRANSACTION given below: 3

Table: ACCOUNT

ACODE	NAME	CITY
D01	PREETI	MUMBAI
D02	SEHER	DELHI
D03	MAULI	DELHI
D04	AASTHA	CHENNAI

Table: TRANSACTION

TID	ACODE	AMOUNT	TTYPE	DOT
101	D01	2500	D	2019-09-02
102	D02	3500	W	2018-01-10
103	D01	2000	D	2019-04-28
104	D03	2800	D	2018-05-20
105	D04	2000	W	2017-07-20
106	D01	5000	D	2017-12-21
107	D03	10000	D	2019-05-19

Note: TType is the Transaction type (where D for deposit and W for withdrawal), DOT is the date of transaction.

(a) SELECT A.ACODE, NAME, AMOUNT, TTYPE
FROM ACCOUNT A, TRANSACTION T

WHERE A.ACODE=T.ACODE AND
CITY NOT IN ('CHENNAI','DELHI');

(b) SELECT DISTINCT ACODE FROM TRANSACTION;

(c) SELECT ACODE, COUNT(*), SUM(AMOUNT)
FROM TRANSACTION GROUP BY ACODE;

37. Evaluate the following postfix notation of expression. Show the status of the stack after every operation. 3

84, 62, –, 14, 3, *, +

OR

Write PUSH(Place) and POP(Place) methods in Python to add Place and remove Place considering them to act as Insert and Delete operations on list of places of the data structure Stack.

SECTION – III

Each question carries 5 marks **(5 × 3 = 15)**

38. Sankalp Skills India Ltd. is a knowledge and skill community which aims to enforce the standards of knowledge and skills in the young generations. It is planning to setup its branches in multiple places with its head office in the nearest city. They have created a model for the setup of their network. 5

As a network administrator, you have to suggest the best network related solutions for their problems raised in (a) to (e) keeping in mind the distances between various locations and other parameters.

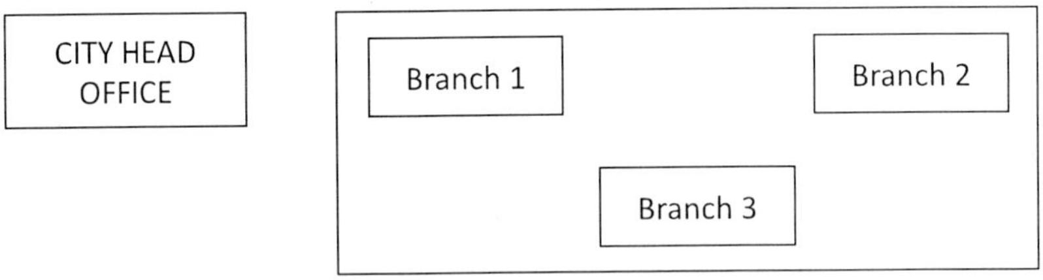

Shortest distance between various locations:

Branch 1 to Branch 2	2 km
Branch 2 to Branch 3	1 km
Branch 1 to Branch 3	1 km
City Head Office to Branch 1	100 km
City Head Office to Branch 2	150 km

Number of computers installed in various locations are as follows:

Branch 1	120
Branch 2	15
Branch 3	26
City Head Office	5

(a) Suggest the most appropriate place to install the server. Justify your answer.

(b) Suggest the best wired medium and draw the cable layout to efficiently connect various locations.

(c) Which hardware device will you suggest to connect all the computers within each branch?

(d) Suggest the type of network out of LAN/ MAN/ WAN to connect the different branches i.e. Branch 1, Branch 2 and Branch 3.

(e) Which service/ protocol will be most helpful to conduct live interactions of experts from head office and people in all other branches?

39. Write SQL commands for the following queries (a) to (e) based on the relations VEHILE and BOOKING tables. 5

Table: VEHICLE		
VCODE	**VTYPE**	**CHARGES**
101	CAR	40
102	SUV	80
103	AC DX BUS	150
104	VOLVO BUS	180

Note: CHARGES is given for Per KM.

Table: BOOKING				
BNO	**NAME**	**TDATE**	**KM**	**VCODE**
B01	Amit Saha	2018-11-12	230	101
B02	Vedika Desai	2018-12-20	120	102
B03	Charu Nayyar	2018-12-28	230	103
B04	Devansh Arora	2019-01-02	530	101
B05	Vijay Ahuja	2019-01-23	120	102

Note: BNO is Booking Number, KM is Kilometer travelled, TDATE is travel date

(a) To display Booking No, Name, TDATE from the table Booking in descending order of TDATE.

(b) To display the details of all the bookings of the person who are travelling by vehicle with code 101 or 102.

(c) To display the BNo and Name of those bookings from the table Booking who travelled in the year 2019 in ascending order of their names.

(d) To display a report with BNO, Name, Amount from tables Booking and Vehicle. Amount is to be calculated as the product of KM and CHARGES.

(e) To display total kilometers travelled by each vehicle type.

40. A binary file "Staff.dat" has the following structure (Scode, Name, Mobile). Write a function Search(N) in Python which takes N as parameter that would search and display the content of a pickled file "Staff.dat", where Name is matching with N. Also, the function would return the total number of Staff with the matching value of N. 5

OR

A binary file "Cinema.dat" has the following structure [MNo, MName, MType].

(a) Write a user defined function CreateMultiplex() to input data for a record and add it to Cinema.dat.

(b) Write a function to search and display all the contents in a pickled file Cinema.dat, where MType is matching with the value 'Comedy'.

Solved Sample Paper – 3 (Theory) - Answers

PART – A

SECTION – I

1. Following can not be used for naming a variable or function:

   (a) Qty*Price (b) class (d) 4no (h) First name

   ½ mark for choosing any two correct options

2. Sub1, Sub2, Sub3 = "Computer Science", "Mathematics","English"

   1 mark for the correct statement declaring strings

3. (a) with open("Story.txt"."r") as f:

   (b) with open("Story.txt" ,"a") as f:

   ½ mark for each correct statement

4. Output:

   CBSE

   1 mark for the correct output

5. Implicit conversion happens when data type conversion is done automatically by Python and is not instructed by the programmer.

   For example:

   ```
   A=10
   B=25.5
   C=A+B
   print(C)
   print(type(C))
   ```

   In this example, the result in C is automatically converted to float value.

   ½ mark for any correct definition of implicit conversion

   ½ mark for any valid example

6. Output: 128

   1 mark for the correct output

7. Identity operators are used to determine whether the value of a variable is of a certain type or not. It is also used to determine whether two variables are referring to the same object or not.

   Two identity operators are:

   (a) is

   (b) is not

   ½ mark for defining identity operator

   ½ mark for writing both the identity operators

8. (a) pickle

(b) os

½ mark for each correct module

9. HTTP

Browsers: Internet Explorer, Google Chrome, Netscape Navigator, Opera, Mozilla Firefox

½ mark for naming the correct protocol
½ mark for any correct browser name

10. Hacker

As hackers aim in correcting security problems and use it in a positive sense. Mr Sanjay informed the CEO of the company regarding the security of their network.

½ mark for choosing the correct option
½ mark for reasoning

11. Domain is the pool of values from which the actual value is choosen.

For example, if there are 10 students in a class and need to assign rollno to each then the domain is 1 to 10 and rollno will be taken for each student from 1 to 10.

½ mark for defining domain
½ mark for any correct example

12. IN operator

1 mark for the correct operator

13. NOW() / DATE() / MONTH() / MONTHNAME() / YEAR() / DAY/ DAYNAME()

½ mark each for any correct function

14. A foreign key is used to represent the relationship between two relations. A foreign key is an attribute whose value is derived from the primary key of another relation.

1 mark for any correct definition of foreign key

15. Computer virus can spread by CDs, pen drive, etc. It is designed to corrupt the host program and gain control over the system without letting the other person know about it.

1 mark for any correct definition of computer virus

16. Divide by 0 is an example of runtime error.

IndexError, NameError are examples of Syntax Error.

½ mark each for the correct example

17. Two iteration statements in Python are

(a) for loop

(b) while loop

½ mark for each correct iteration statement

18. ALTER TABLE Transaction ADD FOREIGN KEY(Acode)

REFERENCES Account(Acode);

½ mark for 1st part of the statement

½ mark for 2nd part of the statement

19. Website is a collection of related web pages which gives information related to a particular topic whereas web page is just like a page from the chapter which gives information related to a sub topic of main topic.

1 mark for any correct difference between website and web page

20. DELETE is a DML statement whereas DROP is a DDL statement.

Delete is used to from the table whereas Drop statement is used to delete the whole table along with its structure.

1 mark for any correct difference between delete and drop

21. URL: https://cbse.nic.in/newsite/index.html

Domain: cbse.nic.in

½ mark for any correct example of URL

½ mark for any correct example of domain from the URL

SECTION – II

22. A video store is about to maintain their video details using SQL to store the data for inventory. As a database administrator, you have decided to declare the following to create the inventory:

- Name of the database – VideoStore
- Name of the table – Video
- The attributes of Video are:

  VCode – character of size 3

  Title – character of size 30 (Not Null constraint)

  Type – character of size 15

  Price – numeric value of type integer

  Qty – numeric value of type integer

Table: Video				
VCode	**Title**	**Type**	**Price**	**Qty**
H01	Dawn of the Dead	Horror	250	3
H02	Evil Dead	Horror	120	2
F01	Interstellar	Fiction	235	4
C01	Caddyshack	Comedy	341	4
H03	The Cabin in the Woods	Horror	225	2
F02	The Invisible Ma	Fiction	346	3

(a) Primary key is VCode as it maintains uniqueness in the table.

1 mark for correct identification of the primary key

(b) CREATE DATABASE VIDEOSTORE;

USE VIDEOSTORE;

½ mark for correct statement of create database
½ mark for correct statement of using database

(c) CREATE TABLE VIDEO(VCode char(3) Primary key,
Title char(15) NOT NULL, Type char(12), Price int, Qty int)

½ mark for the correct first part of the statement
½ mark for the correct second part of the statement

(d) DESC Video;

1 mark for the correct statement

(e) INSERT INTO VIDEO VALUES
("C02", "Hera Pheri", "Comedy", 304, 5)

½ mark for first part of the statement
½ mark for the second part of the statement

23.
```
import csv

def Add_Rec(L):
    with open("order.csv","w",newline='') as C:
        cw=csv.writer(C)
        header=['OrderNo','Prod_ID','Qty','UPrice']
        cw.writerow(header)
        cw.writerow(L)

def Add_More(L):
    with open('order.csv','a',newline='') as C:    #Line 1
        cw=csv.writer(C)
```

```
        cw.writerow(L)                              #Line 2

def Display():
    with open('order.csv','r') as C:
        cr=csv.reader(C)
        for x in cr:                                #Line 3
            print(x)

Add_Rec([1, 'P01', 29, 20])
Add_More([2, 'P02', 10, 100])
Add_More([3, 'P03', 12, 25])
Display()
```

(a) import csv

(b) a

(c) writerow()

(d) cr

(e) ['OrderNo', 'Prod_ID', 'Qty', 'UPrice']
['1', 'P01', '29', '20']
['2', 'P02', '10', '100']
['3', 'P03', '12', '25']

½ mark for any two correct lines of output

PART – B

SECTION – I

24. Explicit conversion, also called type casting which is perform when the programmer forced the conversion from one data type to another. For example: if x=98.45 and then converting float to int by using the statement b=int(x) will discard the decimal value of x and assign only the integer part of x to b.

Explicit type conversion functions in Python are:

int(x) / float(x) / str(x) / chr(x)

1 mark for any correct definition of explicit conversion
½ mark for naming any correct function

25. (a) ASP: Server side script

(b) VB Scripting: Client side script

(c) JSP: Server side script

(d) Java Scripting: Client side script

½ mark for correctly classifying each scripting

OR

Bus topology uses a single cable through which various other devices are connected to the network whereas star topology makes use of central node called hub / switch that connects various devices to the network.

Speed of data transfer is comparatively fast in Star topology than in bus topology.

The fault detection is comparatively easy in Star topology than in bus topology.

1 mark for each correct difference

26. (a) **GSM:** Global System for Mobile Communication

(b) **GPRS:** General Packet Radio Service

(c) **WLL:** Wireless in Local Loop

(d) **WWW:** World Wide Web

½ mark for each correct expansion

27. Break statement – The break statement alters the normal flow of execution as it terminates the current loop and resumes execution of the statement following the loop.

Continue statement – When continue statement is encountered, the control skips the execution of remaining statements inside the body of the loop for the current iteration and jumps to the beginning of the loop for the next iteration.

1 mark for each correct explanation

OR

Range() function – It is a built-in function. It is used to create a list containing a sequence of integers from the given start value upto stop value (excluding the stop value), with a different of the given step value. The start and step parameters are optional. If start is not specified, then it starts with a value 0. If step is not specified, then by default, it is taken as 1.

For example:

```
for I in range(5):
    print(I)
```

Here, I will start from 0 and increment by 1.

So, the output will be 0, 1, 2, 3, 4.

```
for I in range(2, 8, 3):
    print(I)
```

In example, I start from 2 and increment by 3. So, the output will be 2, 5

1 mark for writing range() function
1 mark for explaining it with example

28. Corrected code:

```
for City in ('Delhi', 'Mumbai', 'Calcutta', 'Madras'):
    if City[0]=='M':
        print(City)
```

Line 1 – Errors values of city in quotation mark

Line 1 – Error colon (:) missing at the end of for loop

Line 2 – Error IF is misspelled

Line 2 – Error colon (:) missing at the end of the if statement

29. (a) and (c)

Minimum value for C = 0

Maximum value for C = 2

½ mark for choosing each correct output option
½ mark each for correct minimum and maximum value of C

30. The name of the operation is Cartesian Product (STUDENTxDANCE)

Degree = 4

Cardinality = 6

½ mark for the correct operation name
½ mark each for the correct degree and cardinality

31.

```
import mysql.connector
mydb=mysql.connector.connect(host="localhost",user="root",
                  passwd="root", database="school")   #Line 1

mycursor=mydb.cursor()
s="SELECT * FROM DANCE"                                #Line 2
mycursor.execute(s)
result=mycursor.fetchall()                             #Line 3
print(result)
print("Total number of records: ",mycursor.rowcount)   #Line 4
```

(a) School

(b) Dance

(c) fetchall()

(d) mycursor.rowcount

1 mark for filling each correct blank

32. RDBMS (Relational Database Management System) is used to store data in related tables. Rows and columns of a table are called tuples and attributes respectively. A table is referred to as a relation.

RDBMS software: MySQL, SQL Server, PostgreSQL, Oracle.

1 mark for defining RDBMS
½ mark for each correct RDBMS software

33. Output:

0 A$

1 AB

3 ABC$

6 ABCD

½ mark for each correct line of output

SECTION – II

34.
```
def Prime(N):
    print("Prime numbers 2-",N," : ")
    for I in range(2,N+1):
        f=0
        for J in range(2, I):
            if I%J==0:
                f=1
                break
        if(f==0):
            print(I)

Prime(45)
```

1 mark for the outer for loop to check for numbers from 2 to N
1 mark for inner for loop
1 mark for checking the number is prime or not

35.
```
def Search():
    with open("Places.txt","r") as fin:
        ctr=0
        file=fin.read()
        for f in file.split():
            if len(f)>7:
                print(f,end=' ')
                ctr+=1
        print("\nTotal number of words with length>7: ",ctr)

Search()
```

½ mark for reading the file in correct mode
½ mark for reading the whole file
½ mark for using for loop and splitting the contents word wise
½ mark for comparing the length of the word
½ mark for displaying the word having length >7
½ mark for incrementing the counter and displaying

36. (a)

ACODE	NAME	AMOUNT	TTYPE
D01	PREETI	2500	D
D01	PREETI	2000	D
D01	PREETI	5000	D

1 mark for each correct output

(b)

ACODE
D01
D02
D03
D04

1 mark for each correct output

(c)

ACODE	COUNT(*)	SUM(AMOUNT)
D01	3	9500
D02	1	3500
D03	2	12800
D04	1	2000

1 mark for each correct output

37.

S.No	Value	Operation	Stack status
1	84	Push 84	84
2	62	Push 62	62 84
3	-	- Pop 62 & 84 84-62=22 Push 22	22
4	14	Push 14	14 22
5	3	Push 3	3 14 22
6	*	* Pop 3 & 14 14*3= 42 Push 42	42 22
7	+	+ Pop 42 & 22 22+42=64 Push 64	64

½ mark for showing any two operations

OR

```
def PUSH(Place):
    P=input("Enter the name of the place")
    Place.append(P)
    print(Place)

def POP(Place):
    if len(Place)==0:
        print("Empty List")
    else:
        print(Place.pop()," deleted successfully")
```

½ mark for PUSH header
½ mark for reading the name of the place
1 mark for adding it to the end of the list
½ mark for printing the list

½ mark for POP function header
1 mark for checking the blank list
1 mark for pop operation

SECTION – III

38. (a) Branch 1 is suitable place to install the server as it has maximum number of computers in it.

½ mark for best place to house the server
½ mark for correct justification

(b) Optical Fibre is best wired medium.

STAR TOPOLOGY

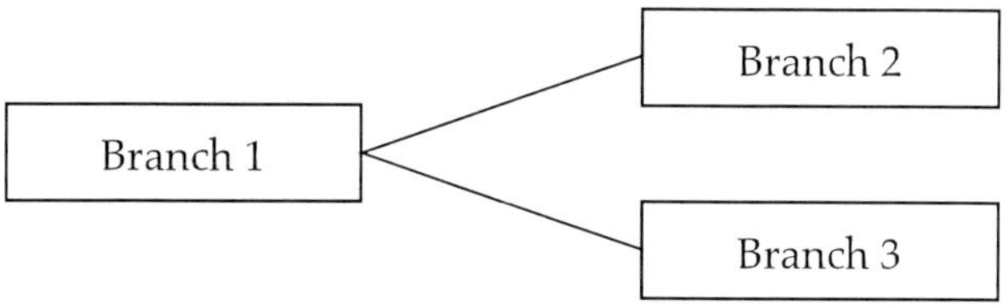

½ mark for the wired medium
½ mark for drawing the layout

(c) Hub / Switch is used to connect all the computers within each branch.

1 mark for writing the correct device

(d) LAN can be used to connect different branches.

1 mark for any correct type of network

(e) VoIP / H3.23 service/ protocol will be most helpful to conduct live interactions of experts from head office and people in all other branches.

1 mark for any correct protocol for live interactions

39. (a) SELECT BNo, Name, TDATE FROM BOOKING
ORDER BY TDATE DESC;

½ mark for first part of the statement
½ mark for second part of the statement

(b) SELECT * FROM BOOKING
WHERE VCODE IN (101, 102);

OR

SELECT * FROM BOOKING WHERE VCODE=101 OR VCODE=102;

½ mark for first part of the query
½ mark for second part of the query

(c) SELECT BNo, Name FROM BOOKING
WHERE YEAR(TDATE)= 2019 ORDER BY NAME;

½ mark for first part of the query
½ mark for second part of the query

(d) SELECT BNO, Name, KM*Charges FROM BOOKING B, VEHICLE V
B.VCODE=V.VCODE;

½ mark for first part of the query
½ mark for second part of the query

(e) SELECT VCODE, SUM(KM) FROM BOOKING
GROUP BY VCODE;

½ mark for first part of the query
½ mark for second part of the query

40.
```
import pickle
def Search(N):
    ctr=0
    with open("Staff.dat","rb") as fin:
        while True:
            try:
                L=pickle.load(fin)
                if N.upper() in L[1].upper():
                    ctr+=1
                    print(L)

            except:
                break
        return ctr


n=input("Enter the name to be searched:")
print("Total no of records matching:",Search(N))
```

½ mark for import pickle and opening the file in correct mode
½ mark for iterating over the records
½ mark for try and except block
1 mark for reading each record
1 mark for comparing the name with the record name
½ mark for displaying the matching record
½ mark for incrementing the counter
½ mark for returning the value of counter

OR

```
import pickle

def CreateMultiplex():
    with open("Cinema.dat","ab") as fout:
        MNo=input("Enter Movie ID")
        MName=input("Enter Movie Name")
        MType=input("Enter Movie Type")
        L=[MNo,MName,MType]
        pickle.dump(L,fout)

def Search():
    with open("Cinema.dat","rb") as fin:
        while True:
            try:
                L=pickle.load(fin)
                if L[2]=='Comedy':
                    print(L)
            except:
                break
```

(a)

½ mark for import pickle

½ mark for opening the file in correct mode

½ mark for reading the contents of the members in a list

½ mark for adding values to the list

½ mark for writing it in the pickled file

(b)

½ mark for opening the file in correct mode

½ mark for while loop

½ mark for try – except block

½ mark for reading each object

½ mark for comparing the type as comedy and printing

Solved Sample Paper – 4 (Theory)

M.M.: 70 **Time: 3 hrs**

General Instructions

1. This question paper contains two parts A and B. Each part is compulsory.
2. Both Part A and Part B have choices.
3. Part-A has 2 sections:
   a. Section – I is short answer questions, to be answered in one word or one line.
   b. Section – II has two case studies questions. Each case study has 4 case-based subparts. An examinee is to attempt any 4 out of the 5 subparts.
4. Part - B is Descriptive Paper.
5. Part- B has three sections
   a. Section-I is short answer questions of 2 marks each in which two question have internal options.
   b. Section-II is long answer questions of 3 marks each in which two questions have internal options.
   c. Section-III is very long answer questions of 5 marks each in which one question has internal option.
6. All programming questions are to be answered using Python Language only.

PART – A

SECTION – I

Attempt any 15 questions from question numbers 1 to 21. Each question carries 1 mark. **(1 × 15 = 15 marks)**

1. Define keyword. Write any two examples of keyword. 1

2. Give the output of following: 1

X = 3

X + = X – X

print(X)

3. Write a statement in Python to open a text file ARTICLE.TXT so that new contents can be added to the end of file. 1

4. Name the function/ method used for: 1

(a) Finding second occurrence of m in malyalam.

(b) Get the position of an item in the list

5. How does method write() different from writelines()? 1

6. Write the names of the immutable data objects from the following: 1

(a) Tuple (b) List (c) String (d) Dictionary

7. Which of the options out of (a) to (d) is the correct data type for the variable Vowels as defined in the following Python statement? 1

Vowels=('a', 'e', 'i', 'o', 'u')

(a) Dictionary (b) Array (c) Tuple (d) List

8. Name the Python Library modules which need to be imported to invoke the following functions: 1

(a) ceil() (b) randint()

9. Which protocol is used to have an audio-video chat with an expert sitting far away to resolve a technical issue? 1

10. Aaliyah is expected to write a research paper on a given topic by her teacher. She had a brother who took a similar class five years ago. She asked his brother for a copy of his paper and then takes the paper and submits the entire paper as her own research work. 1

Which of the following activity appropriately categorises the act of Aaliyah?

(a) Phishing (b) Virus (c) Plagiarism (d) Spamming

11. Which SQL command and clause is used to add a new attribute in a table? 1

12. In SQL, name the two wildcards used in conjunction with the LIKE operator. 1

13. Which SQL aggregate function is used to count all records of a table? 1

14. Write the full form of the following abbreviations: 1

(a) DDL (b) DML

15. An organisation purchases new electronic gadgets every year and dumps the old ones into the local dumping yard. Write the name of the most appropriate category of waste that the organisation is creating every year, out of the following options: 1

(a) Solid waste (b) E-waste

(c) Commercial waste (d) Business waste 1

16. Write the output of the following Python code: 1

```
for A in range(3, 9, 3):
    print(A*'#')
```

17. List any one similarity and one difference between List and Dictionary. 1

18. Differentiate between WHERE and HAVING clause. 1

19. Define Firewall. 1

20. Which clause is used to work on a group of rows to perform some action? 1

21. Identify the domain name and URL from the following: 1
http://cbseacademic.nic.in/SQP_CLASSXII_2020-21.html

SECTION – II

Consists of case study questions and are compulsory to attempt. Attempt any 4 sub parts from each question. Each sub part carries 1 mark. (4 + 4 = 8 marks)

22. Serbia University is about to maintain their courses using SQL to store it in the inventory. As a database administrator, you have decided to declare the following to create the inventory:

- Name of the database – SUNIVERSITY
- Name of the table – Courses
- The attribute of Course are:
  CID – character of size 3
  CNAME – character of size 15
  FEES – numeric value of type integer

Table: COURSE

CID	CNAME	FEES
C11	COMPUTER SECURITY	22000
C12	COMPUTER NETWORK	15000
C13	INFORMATION TECHNOLOGY	12000
C14	PYTHON	9800
C15	JAVASCRIPT	5500

(a) Identify the most appropriate attribute for primary key. 1

(b) Write SQL statement to add primary key to the existing relation. 1

(c) While creating the relation, you have given the size for CNAME as 15 and then realised that the CNAME field has to change the size limit from 15 to 20. Write SQL statement to change the size limit for CNAME. 1

(d) Once you have created the above mentioned table with all the data in it. You wanted to add one more attribute to the table named Mobile with character length of 10. Write SQL statement to perform this change. 1

(e) Write SQL query to add default value for FEES as 5000. 1

23. Paarth wants to create a csv file "Student.csv" which contains the student details such as RollNo, Name and Section of his batch mates. He has written the following code so as to add more records, display all the records and delete a record using rollno. As a programmer, help him to fill in the blanks to run the code effectively.

```
import csv
import os
def Add_St(L):
    with open("___________","a",newline='') as a:    #Line 1
        c=csv.writer(a)
        c.writerow(L)
def Display():
    with open("Student.csv",'r') as c:
        cw=csv.________(c)                         #Line 2
        for x in cw:
            print(x)
def DelSel(r):
    l=[]
    flag=0
    with open('Student.csv','r') as a:
        c=csv.reader(a)
        for x in c:
            l.append(x)
            if x[0]==____(r):                     #Line 3
                l.remove(x)
                flag=1
    with open('temp.csv','w',newline='') as b:
        d=csv.writer(b)
        d.__________(l)                          #Line 4
    if flag==0:
        print("Not found")
    else:
        print("deleted successfully")
    os.remove('Student.csv')
    os.rename('temp.csv','Student.csv')

L1=[1,"Abhay","A"]
L2=[2,"Arpita","B"]
L3=[3,"Sujatha","A"]
Add_St(L1)
Add_St(L2)
Add_St(L3)
DelSel(2)
Display()
```

(a) Which file needs to be opened to fill in the blank for Line 1? 1

(b) Write the csv method to fetch the data from the file for Line 2? 1

(c) Which function needs to be filled in for the blank in Line 3? 1

(d) Write the name of the method of csv to write a record in the file to fill in the blank in Line 4? 1

(e) Write the output of the program while executing the code. 1

PART - B

SECTION – I

Each question carries 2 marks **(2 × 10 = 20)**

24. Evaluate the following expressions: 2

(a) 1 + 13 – 5 < 6 / 3 * 5 (b) 12 * 2 + (20 – 4) / 4

25. Define IOT. Also, write any two examples of IOT. 2

26. Write the full form of the following: 2

(a) VoIP (b) MAC (c) URI (d) DNS

27. Write any four advantages of writing program using functions. 2

28. Rewrite the following code in Python after removing all syntax error(s). Underline each correction done in the code. 2

```
val=int(input("Enter a value"))
sum=0
for c in range(1,val,3)
    sum+=c
    if c%2==0:
        Print(c*10)
    Else:
        print(c*)
print(sum)
```

29. What possible output(s) are expected to be displayed on screen at the time of execution of the program from the following code? Also specify the maximum values that can be assigned to each of the variables START and END. 2

```
import random

pts=[20,30,40,10,25,90]
Start=random.randint(1,3)
End=random.randint(2, 5)
print(Start, End,end=' ')
for x in range(Start, End):
    print(pts[x],end='#')
```

(a) 20#30# (b) 25#90# (c) 30# (d) 30#40#10#

30. Define Degree and Cardinality. Based upon given table, write degree and cardinality. 2

BookID	Title	Author	Price
B01	Harry Potter	J. K. Rowling	2325
B02	Panchtantra	Vishnu Sharma	595

31. Charvi has written the Python code to fetch the information from SQL database named SCHOOL to display all the records from the table STUDENT where name is ending with 'a'. Also, she wants to display the total number of records having 'a' as a last character in their names. 2

You as a programmer, help her to fill in the statements so as to get the desired result.

```
import mysql.connector
mydb=mysql.connector.________(host="localhost",user="root",          #Line 1
                             passwd="root", database="school")

mycursor=mydb.cursor()
s="SELECT * FROM STUDENT WHERE NAME ________"                       #Line 2
mycursor.________(s)                                                 #Line 3
result=mycursor.fetchall()
print(result)
print("Total number of records: ",________.rowcount)                #Line 4
```

(a) Fill in the blank for Line 1

(b) Complete the SQL query in the blank given in Line 2 to get the records where name ends with 'a'.

(c) Write the method to run the query in Line 3.

(d) Fill in the blank in Line 4.

32. Differentiate between Selection and Projection operations in context of a Relational database with the help of an example. 2

33. Find and write the output of the following python code: 2

```
def Change(P, Q=5):
    P=P/Q
    Q=P%Q
    print(P, "#", Q)
    return P

A=45
B=5
A=Change(A,B)
print(A, "&", B)
B=Change(B)
print(A, "&",B)
```

SECTION – II

Each question carries 3 marks **(3 × 4 = 12)**

34. Write a user defined function ZeroEnding(Marks) to add all those values in the list of Marks, which are ending with zero (0) and display the sum. 3

For example: If the Marks contain [90, 82, 45, 80, 67, 29, 40]

The sum should be displayed as 210

35. Charvi has created a text file using a text editor and saved it as "Story.txt". After saving she realised that she wrongly typed alphabet J in place of I everywhere in the document. 3

Write a function Change() in Python that would display the corrected version of the entire content of the file "Story.txt" by replacing "J" with "I".

36. Write outputs for SQL queries (a) to (c) which are based on the following tables, Customer and Purchase: 3

Table: Customer		
Code	**Name**	**City**
C01	Sakshi	New Delhi
C02	Charu	Mumbai
C03	Chetna	Mumbai
C04	Mohini	New Delhi

Table: Purchase			
No	**P_Date**	**Qty**	**Code**
1	2019-10-22	3	C01
2	2019-12-25	10	C02
3	2020-01-20	45	C01
4	2020-02-15	34	C01
5	2020-02-25	35	C03
6	2020-02-28	20	C01
7	2020-03-02	10	C02

(a) SELECT COUNT(DISTINCT CODE) FROM PURCHASE;

(b) SELECT SUM(QTY), CODE FROM PURCHASE GROUP BY CODE;

(c) SELECT NAME, QTY, P_DATE FROM PURCHASE, CUSTOMER
WHERE PURCHASE.CODE = CUSTOMER.CODE AND QTY IN (10, 20, 30);

37. Convert the following infix expression to its equivalent Postfix expression, showing the stack contents for each step of conversion. 3

P + (Q – R) * S / T

OR

Write AddClient(Client) function in Python to add a new Client to a list of Client Names considering it to act as an insert operation of the stack data structure. Also, write DeleteClient() function in Python to delete a client from a list of Client Names, considering it to act as delete operation of the stack data structure.

SECTION – III

Each question carries 5 marks **(5 × 3 = 15)**

38. Arpita Training Educational Institute is setting up its centre in Ahmedabad with four specialised departments for Oncology, Orthopaedic, Paediatric and Nephrology along with an administrative office in separate buildings. The physical distance between these department buildings and the number of computers to be installed in these departments are given as follows. 5

You as a network expert, have to answer the queries that are raised in parts (a) to (e).

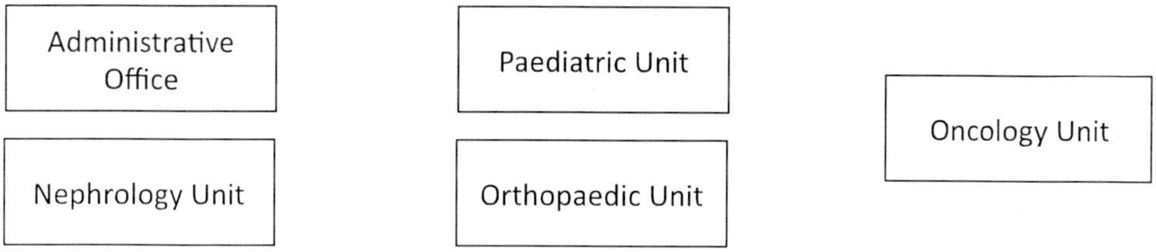

Shortest distance between various locations in metres:

Administrative Office to Nephrology Unit	25
Nephrology Unit to Orthopaedic Unit	35
Paediatric Unit to Administrative Office	30
Orthopaedic Unit to Paediatric Unit	30
Administrative Office to Orthopaedic Unit	60
Oncology Unit to Orthopaedic Unit	55
Administrative Office to Oncology Unit	120

Number of computers installed at various units are as follows:

Oncology Unit	34
Orthopaedic Unit	45
Nephrology Unit	40
Paediatric Unit	30
Administrative Office	120

(a) Suggest the most suitable place to install the main server of this institution to get efficient connectivity. Give justification.

(b) Suggest the best cable layout for effective network connectivity of the units.

(c) Suggest the device to be installed in each unit for connecting computers installed within the unit.

(d) Suggest the placement of repeater with justification.

(e) Suggest the topology of network and network cable for efficiently connecting each computer installed in each of the units out of the following:

Topologies: Bus Topology, Star Topology

Network Cable: Twisted Pair Cable, Coaxial Cable, Ethernet Cable

39. Write SQL commands for the following queries (a) to (e) based on the relations Product and Client 5

Table: PRODUCT

PCode	Item	Manufacturer	Price
F001	Face Wash	Dove	210
S001	Soap	Dove	80
F002	Face Wash	Himalaya	195
S002	Soap	Himalaya	95

Table: Client

CID	Name	City	PCode	Qty
1	Sarita	New Delhi	F001	120
2	Shalini	Mumbai	F002	100
3	Annu	New Delhi	S001	200
4	Balwinder	New Delhi	F001	250

(a) To display the details of all those clients whose city is New Delhi.

(b) To decrease the price of all products by 5%.

(c) To display Client ID, Name, Amount from table Client and Product with their corresponding PCode.. Amount is to be calculated as Qty*Price.

(d) To display the details of those clients whose Name starts with S.

(e) To display the sum of quantity city wise from table Client.

40. A binary file "DOCS.DAT" has structure [DID, Name, Specialisation]. 5

(a) Write a user defined function NewDr() to input data for a record of Doctor and add it to DOCS.DAT.

(b) Write a function SPLDOCS() to search and display the contents from a pickled file DOCS.DAT, where Specialisation of Doctors is 'Paediatrics'.

OR

A binary file "Stock.dat" has structure (ItemCode, Name, Price, Qty).

(a) Write a function STOCK() in Python that would search and display Name and Price from a pickled file "Stock.dat", where Quantity of items are less than 5.

(b) Write a function SEARCH(N) in Python where N is passed as a parameter to search and display all the records matching the Name of the items from "Stock.dat" with the parameter N.

Solved Sample Paper – 4 (Theory) - Answers

PART – A

SECTION – I

1. Keyword is a reserved word. It cannot be used to name variables, functions. It is predefined and the definition for keyword is already defined with the interpreter. For example: True, False, class, finally, return, None, for, try, except

   ½ mark for any correct definition of keyword
   ½ mark for any two correct examples of keyword

2. Output: 3

   1 mark for the correct output

3. with open("ARTICLE.TXT","a") as fout:

   Or

   fout=open("ARTICLE.TXT","a")

   1 mark for writing the correct python statement

4. (a) find / str.find("m",1)
   (b) index()

   ½ mark each for the correct method

5. Write() is used to write a single string at a time whereas writelines() is used to write a list of strings.

   1 mark for any correct difference

6. (a) Tuple and (c) String

   ½ mark for choosing each correct option

7. (c) Tuple

   1 mark for choosing the correct option

8. (a) math
   (b) random

   ½ mark for each correct libray / module

9. VoIP / H.323 protocol

   1 mark for the correct answer

10. (c) Plagiarism

    1 mark for choosing the correct option

11. ALTER TABLE command ADD clause

    ½ mark for command and ½ mark for clause

12. The two wildcards used in conjunction with the LIKE operator are underscore (_) and percent (%) symbol.

½ mark for each correct wildcard

13. COUNT(*)

1 mark for the correct function

14. DDL: Data Definition Language

DML: Data Manipulation Language

½ mark for each correct full form

15. (b) E-waste

1 mark for choosing the correct option

16. Output:

```
###
######
```

½ mark for each correct line of output

17. Both are mutable data types.

List is a sequential data type i.e. they are indexed whereas dictionary is a mapping data type which consists of key-value pairs.

½ mark for any correct similarity
½ mark for any correct difference

18. Where is used to put a condition in SQL command whereas Having is used to put the condition when Group by command is used in SQL.

1 mark for any correct difference

19. A firewall is a network security device that monitors incoming and outgoing network traffic and security rules can be set to permit or block the data packets.

1 mark for any correct definition of firewall

20. Group by clause

1 mark for the correct clause/command

21. Domain: cbseacademic.nic.in

URL: http://cbseacademic.nic.in/SQP_CLASSXII_2020-21.html

½ mark each for the correct answer

SECTION – II

22. (a) CID

1 mark for the correct primary key

(b) ALTER TABLE COURSE
ADD PRIMARY KEY (CID);

½ mark for first part of the query
½ mark for second part of the query

(c) ALTER TABLE COURSE
MODIFY CNAME CHAR(40);

OR

ALTER TABLE COURSE
MODIFY CNAME VARCHAR(40);

½ mark for first part of the query
½ mark for second part of the query

(d) ALTER TABLE COURSE
ADD MOBILE CHAR(10);

OR

ALTER TABLE COURSE
ADD MOBILE VARCHAR(10);

½ mark for first part of the query
½ mark for second part of the query

(e) ALTER TABLE COURSE
MODIFY FEES INTEGER DEFAULT 5000;

½ mark for first part of the query
½ mark for second part of the query

23.
```
import csv
import os
def Add_St(L):
    with open("Student.csv",'a',newline='') as a:
        c=csv.writer(a)
        c.writerow(L)
def Display():
    with open("Student.csv",'r') as c:
        cw=csv.reader(c)
        for x in cw:
            print(x)
def DelSel(r):
    l=[]
    flag=0
    with open('Student.csv','r') as a:
        c=csv.reader(a)
        for x in c:
            l.append(x)
            if x[0]==str(r):
                l.remove(x)
                flag=1
    with open('temp.csv','w',newline='') as b:
        d=csv.writer(b)
        d.writerows(l)
```

```
    if flag==0:
        print("Not found")
    else:
        print("deleted successfully")
    os.remove('Student.csv')
    os.rename('temp.csv','Student.csv')

L1=[1,"Abhay","A"]
L2=[2,"Arpita","B"]
L3=[3,"Sujatha","A"]
Add_St(L1)
Add_St(L2)
Add_St(L3)
DelSel(2)
Display()
```

(a) Student.csv

1 mark for mentioning the correct file name

(b) reader

1 mark for mentioning the reader method

(c) str(r)

1 mark for str function

(d) writerows()

1 mark for the correct method/function

(e) Output:

deleted successfully

['1', 'Abhay', 'A']

['3', 'Sujatha', 'A']

1 mark for the correct output

PART - B

SECTION – I

24. (a) True

(b) 28.0

1 mark for each correct output

25. IOT is Internet Of Things which refers to a collection of interconnected devices that communicate with other devices without human intervention. For example, autonomous cars, smart appliances, wearable tech.

1 mark for any correct definition of IOT

½ mark for each correct example

26. (a) **VOIP:** Voice Over Internet Protocol
 (b) **MAC:** Media Access Control
 (c) **URL:** Uniform Resource Identifier
 (d) **DNS:** Domain Name System

½ mark each for the correct full form

27. Advantages of using functions in the program are:
 - Increases readability, particularly for longer code as by using functions, the program is better organised and easy to understand.
 - Reduces code length as same code is not required to be written at multiple places in a program.
 - It also makes debugging easier.
 - Increases reusability, as function can be called from another function or another program. Thus, we can reuse or build upon already defined functions and avoid repetitions of writing the same piece of code.
 - Work can be easily divided among team members and completed in parallel.

½ mark for each correct advantage

28. **Corrected Code:**

```
val=int(input("Enter a value"))
sum=0
for c in range(1,val,3):
    sum+=c
    if c%2==0:
        print(c*10)
    else:
        print(c*2)
print(sum)
```

½ mark for each correction and underlining the correction

29. Correct output options are:
 (c) 30#
 (d) 30#40#10#
 Maximum value assigned to Start = 3
 Maximum value assigned to End=5

½ mark for choosing each correct option
½ mark for writing each correct maximum value

30. Degree is the total number of attributes in a relation and Cardinality is the total number of tuples in a relation.
 Degree=4
 Cardinality = 2

½ mark each for correct definition of degree and cardinality
½ mark for mentioning the correct output

31. Code:

```
import mysql.connector
mydb=mysql.connector.connect(host="localhost",user="root",
                              passwd="root",database="school")
mycursor=mydb.cursor()
s="SELECT * FROM STUDENT WHERE NAME LIKE '%a'"
mycursor.execute(s)
result=mycursor.fetchall()
print(result)
print("Total number of records: ",mycursor.rowcount)
```

(a) connect()

(b) LIKE 'a%'

(c) execute()

(d) mycursor

½ mark for filling each blank correctly

32. Selection is the selecting the required tuples from the relation whereas Projection operation is used to take the required attributes from the relation.

For example, when we write the query to select certain records / tuples on some criteria then it is an example of Selection operation.

SELECT * FROM STUDENT WHERE RNO>10;

When we just want to display particular columns for all the records then it is an example of Projection operation.

SELECT RNO, NAME FROM STUDENT;

1 mark for any correct difference
1 mark for any correct example

33. Output:

9.0 # 4.0

9.0 & 5

1.0 # 1.0

9.0 & 1.0

½ mark for each correct line of output

SECTION – II

34.
```
def ZeroEnding(Marks):
    s=0
    for i in Marks:
        if i%10==0:
            s+=i
    print(s)
```

½ mark for initialising sum variable as 0
1 mark using for loop
1 mark for checking the last digit 0
½ mark for adding it to the variable and display

35.
```
def Change():
    with open('Story.txt','r')as fin:
        a=fin.read()
        for ch in a:
            if ch in 'jJ':
                print('i',end='')
            else:
                print(ch,end='')
```

½ mark for opening the file in correct mode
½ mark for reading all the contents of the file
½ mark using for loop
½ mark for checking each character
½ mark for printing I in place of j
½ mark for printing other characters as it is

36. (a) COUNT(DISTINCT CODE)
3

1 mark for the correct output

(b)

SUM(QTY)	CODE
102	C01
20	C02
35	C03

1 mark for the correct output

(c)

NAME	QTY	P_DATE
Charu	10	2019-12-25
Sakshi	20	2020-02-28
Charu	10	2020-03-02

1 mark for the correct output

37. P + (Q – R) * S / T
[P + (((Q – R) * S) / T)]

Symbol scanning	Stack	Postfix expression
[	[	-
P	[	P
+	[+	P
(	[+ (	P

Symbol scanning	Stack	Postfix expression
(	[+((	P
(	[+(((	P
Q	[+(((	PQ
-	[+(((-	PQ
R	[+(((-	PQR
)	[+((	PQR-
*	[+((*	PQR-
S	[+((*	PQR–S
)	[+(	PQR–S*
/	[+(/	PQR–S*
T	[+(/	PQR–S*T
)	[+	PQR–S*T/
]	NULL	PQR–S*T/+

1 mark if the final output is given without mentioning each step

OR

```
def AddClient(Client):
    N=input("Enter the name of the Client")
    Client.append(N)
    print(Client)

def DeleteClient():
    if len(Client)==0:
        print("Empty List")
    else:
        print(Client.pop()," deleted successfully")
```

1 mark for adding the name of client
½ mark for displaying the list of clients after adding
½ mark for checking the empty list
1 mark for deleting and displaying the data

SECTION – III

38. (a) The most suitable place to install the main server of this institution to get efficient connectivity is Administrative Office because it has maximum number of computers in it.

½ mark for correct placement
½ mark for the justification

(b) Star Topology

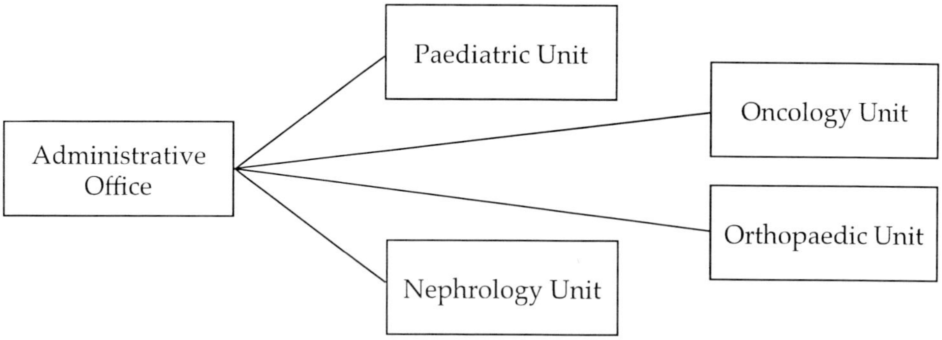

1 mark for the layout and topology

(b) Hub / Switch will be installed in each unit for connecting computers installed within the unit.

1 mark for the correct answer

(c) Repeater will be placed between Administrative Office and Oncology unit as the distance between them is more than 75 mts.

½ mark for the correct placement
½ mark for any correct justification

(d) Topologies: Star Topology

Network Cable: Ethernet Cable

½ mark for choosing the correct topology
½ mark for choosing the correct network cable

39. (a) SELECT * FROM CLIENT

WHERE CITY = 'NEW DELHI';

½ mark for first part of the query
½ mark for second part of the query

(b) UPDATE PRODUCT SET PRICE=PRICE – PRICE*5/100;

1 mark for the correct SQL statement

(c) SELECT CID, Name, Qty*Price FORM CLIENT, PRODUCT

WHERE CLIENT.PCode=PRODUCT.PCode;

½ mark for first part of the query
½ mark for second part of the query

(d) SELECT * FROM CLIENT

WHERE NAME LIKE 'S%';

½ mark for first part of the query
½ mark for second part of the query

(e) SELECT CITY, SUM(QTY) FROM CLIENT

GROUP BY CITY;

½ mark for first part of the query
½ mark for second part of the query

40. (a)
```
import pickle
def NewDr():
    with open("DOCS.dat","ab") as fout:
        ID=input("Enter Doctor ID")
        Name=input("Enter Name")
        S=input("Enter Specialisation")
        L=[ID,Name,S]
        pickle.dump(L,fout)
```

½ mark for import pickle
½ mark for opening the file in correct mode
1 mark for reading the data in a list
½ mark for writing it into the data file

(b)
```
def SPLDOCS():
    with open("DOCS.dat","rb") as fin:
        while True:
            try:
                L=pickle.load(fin)
                if L[2].lower()=='paediatrics':
                    print(L)
            except:
                break
```

½ mark for opening the file in correct mode
½ mark for try and except block
½ mark for reading a record
½ mark for checking the condition
½ mark for display statement

OR

(a)
```
import pickle
def STOCK():
    with open("Stock.dat","rb") as fin:
        print("List of items less than 5 are: ")
        while True:
            try:
                L=pickle.load(fin)
                if L[3]<5:
                    print(L)
            except:
                break
```

½ mark for import
½ mark for opening the file in correct mode
½ mark for try and except block
½ mark for reading a record
½ mark for checking the condition and displaying

(b)
```
def SEARCH(N):
    with open("Stock.dat","rb") as fin:
        while True:
            try:
                L=pickle.load(fin)
                if L[1].lower() in N.lower():
                    print(L)
            except:
                break
```

½ mark for opening the file in correct mode
½ mark for try and except block
½ mark for reading a record
½ mark for checking the condition
½ mark for display statement

Solved Sample Paper – 5 (Theory)

M.M.: 70 **Time: 3 hrs**

General Instructions

1. This question paper contains two parts A and B. Each part is compulsory.
2. Both Part A and Part B have choices.
3. Part-A has 2 sections:
   a. Section – I is short answer questions, to be answered in one word or one line.
   b. Section – II has two case studies questions. Each case study has 4 case-based subparts. An examinee is to attempt any 4 out of the 5 subparts.
4. Part - B is Descriptive Paper.
5. Part- B has three sections
   a. Section-I is short answer questions of 2 marks each in which two question have internal options.
   b. Section-II is long answer questions of 3 marks each in which two questions have internal options.
   c. Section-III is very long answer questions of 5 marks each in which one question has internal option.
6. All programming questions are to be answered using Python Language only.

PART - A

SECTION – I

Attempt any 15 questions from question numbers 1 to 21. Each question carries 1 mark. **(1 × 15 = 15 marks)**

1. Which of the following are keywords in Python? 1

(a) try (b) range (c) FOR (d) True

2. Which of the following is not a valid variable name in Python? Justify reason for it not being a valid name. 1

(a) Area (b) _Area (c) 4Area (d) Area_

3. Consider the following code and give the output: 1

```
f=open("test.txt","r+")
f.write("hello everyone")
print(f.tell())
f.seek(6,0)
print(f.read(4))
f.close()
```

4. Write the type of tokens from the following: 1

(a) Roll_no (b) if

5. Which of the following is a valid logical operator in Python? 1

(a) // (b) ? (c) and (d) =

6. Write a statement in Python to declare a dictionary whose keys are 301, 041, 042 and values English, Mathematics and Physics respectively. 1

7. Write the output of the following Python code: 1

```
T1=(3,4,6,9,23,2)
print(T1[3:5])
```

8. Name the Python Library modules which need to be imported to invoke the following functions: 1

(a) factorial() (b) writerow()

9. Name the protocol: 1

(a) Used to transfer voice using packet switched network.

(b) Used for chatting between 2 groups or between 2 individuals.

10. Criminals access someone's computer and encrypt the user's personal files and data. The user is unable to access this data unless they pay the criminals to decrypt the files. Which type of Cyber threat is it? 1

11. Which command in SQL is used to modify the records of the table? 1

12. In SQL, what is the use of NOT NULL constraint? 1

13. Which keyword is used to sort the records of a table in descending order? 1

14. Choose the DML command(s) from the following: 1

(a) DELETE (b) CREATE (c) UPDATE (d) DROP

15. Which transmission media cables carry data signals in the form of light and are secure mode of data transmission? 1

16. Define String in Python. 1

17. Write the output of the following Python code: 1

```
Line = 'Learning Python is fun'
L = Line.split()
print(L)
```

18. Define Foreign key. 1

19. Write the importance of cookies. 1

20. Write the use of DBMS. 1

21. Define IP Address. 1

SECTION – II

Consists of case study questions and are compulsory to attempt. Attempt any 4 sub parts from each question. Each sub part carries 1 mark. (4 + 4 = 8 marks)

22. Consider the following table:

Table: RESULT			
ST_ID	**NAME**	**EXAMID**	**MARKS**
1001	Abhimanyu	1	48
1001	Abhimanyu	2	74
1002	Mihir	1	65
1003	Devanh	1	33
1003	Devanh	2	56

(a) Write SQL statement to create the table RESULT. 1

(b) Srishti wants to know the number of students who took the test. She writes the following SQL statement to count the Student ID without duplicates. However, her output is not coming correct. Rewrite the statement to get the count of unique student ids.

SELECT DISTINCT (COUNT ST_ID) FROM RESULT; 1

(c) Write SQL statement to create another table STUDENT with fields ST_ID, Name, Class, Section where ST_ID is a primary key. 1

(d) Write SQL statement to add a new attribute MOBILE to the STUDENT table. 1

(e) The spelling of name "Devanh" is written wrong in the RESULT table. Write SQL statement to write it "Devansh". 1

23. Kavita created the python program to work with csv file "Book.csv" which contains the book id, book name and price of the books. Help her to fill up the blanks to execute the program successfully.

```
import csv
import _____                                  #Line 1
def Add_Book(L):
    with open("Book.csv",'a',newline='') as a:
        c=csv._________(a)                    #Line 2
        c.writerow(L)
def Display():
    with open("Book.csv",'r') as c:
        cw=csv.reader(c)
        for x in _____:                       #Line 3
            print(x)
def DelSel(r):
    l=[]
    flag=0
    with open('Book.csv','r') as a:
        c=csv.reader(a)
        for x in c:
            l.append(x)
            if x[0]==str(r):
                l._________(x)                   #Line 4
                flag=1
    with open('temp.csv','w',newline='') as b:
        d=csv.writer(b)
        d.writerows(l)
    if flag==0:
        print("Not found")
    else:
        print(r, "deleted successfully")
    os.remove('Book.csv')
    os.rename('temp.csv','Book.csv')
L1=[1,"NCERT Maths 8",150]
L2=[2,"NCERT Science 8",180]
L3=[3,"NCERT Maths 9",180]
Add_Book(L1)
Add_Book(L2)
Add_Book(L3)
DelSel(3)
Display()
```

(a) Which module is to be imported in Line 1? 1

(b) Write the name of the method in Line 2. 1

(c) Fill in the correct name in Line 3. 1

(d) Write the name of the method to delete the record. 1

(e) Write the output of the program while executing the code. 1

PART - B

SECTION – I

Each question carries 2 marks **(2 × 10 = 20)**

24. Evaluate the following expressions: 2

(a) 15 / 4 + (8 + 3.0) (b) 2 ** (2 + 1)

25. Write any two ways to make sure that the data is secure and is available only to the intended and authorized persons in a network. 2

26. Write the expanded form for: 2

(a) NIC (b) MAN (c) ISP (d) IP

27. Explain try..except block with the help of user defined function def divide(x, y) which raises an error when the denominator is zero while dividing x by y and displays the quotient otherwise. 2

28. Rewrite the following code in Python after removing all syntax error(s). Underline each correction done in the code. 2

```
20=A
for B in range(0, A)
     IF B%3==0:
          print(B*3)
     Else:
          print(B+3)
```

29. What are the possible output(s) expected from the following Python code? Also, specify the maximum and minimum value of x. 2

```
import random

str='Python'
i=0
while str[i]!='o':
     x=random.randint(0,3)+2
     print(str[x],'-',end='')
     i=i+1
```

(a) P-y-t-h- (b) n-h-n-h (c) n-o-n-t (d) P-h-o-n

30. Given the following table Restaurant: 2

Table: Restaurant			
ICode	**Item**	**Qty**	**Price**
1	Gulab Jamun	200	20
2	Burfi	NULL	120
3	Rasgulla	100	25

Write the output of the following statements:

(a) SELECT AVG(Qty) FROM Restaurant;

(b) SELECT COUNT(Qty) FROM Restaurant;

31. Which of the following are valid Cursor methods used to retrieve the SQL query results and execute SQL statements? 2

(a) Cursor.fetchone()

(b) Cursor.fetchmany()

(c) Cursor.fetchall()

(d) Cursor.run()

(e) Cursor.execute()

32. Herman is using the following SQL statement to delete a row for EmpID=201 from the table EMPLOYEE: 2

DROP EMPLOYEE WHERE EmpID EQUALS 201;

He is getting error. Help Herman by rewriting the correct statement.

33. Find the output of the following program: 2

```
def calc():
    i=8
    while i>1:
        if(i%2==0):
            a=i%2
            i=i-1
        else:
            i=i-2
            a=i
        print(a**2)

calc()
```

SECTION – II

Each question carries 3 marks **(3 × 4 = 12)**

34. Write a user defined function arrange(A) which accepts A as an argument of a list of integers and sets all the negative elements to the left and all positive elements to the right side of the list. 3

For example, if List=[2, -3, 1, -9, -5, 8],

then the output should be: [-3, -9, -5, 2, 1, 8]

35. Write a user defined function Show_caps() in python to read the content of a text file "Notes.txt" and display the entire content in capital letters. Example, if the file contains: 3

"This is some sample data"

Then the function should display the output as:

THIS IS SOME SAMPLE DATA

36. Consider the following tables PATIENT AND TEST. Write the output for the questions (a) to (c): 3

Table: PATIENT

PID	NAME	ADMISSION	TESTID
P01	Suraj	2019-12-20	T01
P02	Tina	2020-01-18	T05
P03	Mitesh	2020-03-13	T05
P04	Roopesh	2020-03-20	T03
P05	Pratibha	2020-03-23	T05

Table: TEST

TESTID	TESTNAME	COST
T01	MALARIA	340
T02	HAEMOGLOBIN	150
T03	PLATELET COUNT	1500
T04	TYPHOID	500
T05	COVID	4500

(a) SELECT DISTINCT(TESTID) FROM PATIENT;

(b) SELECT TESTID, COUNT(*) FROM PATIENT GROUP BY TESTID;

(c) SELECT NAME FROM PATIENT WHERE NAME LIKE "%a%";

37. Write PushOn(Book) and PopOut(Book) methods/ functions in Python to a new book and delete a book from a list of book titles, considering them to act as push and pop operations of the Stack data structure. 3

SECTION – III

Each question carries 5 marks **(5 × 3 = 15)**

38. NewGen Public School is setting up the network between different buildings of school campus. There are four buildings named as SENIOR, MIDDLE, JUNIOR AND ADMIN. 5

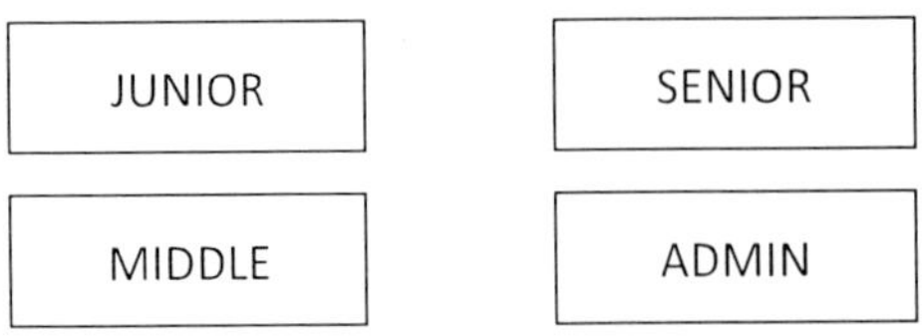

Distance between various buildings are given below (in mtrs):

Junior to Middle	35
Middle to Senior	110
Senior to Junior	70
Admin to Senior	30
Admin to Junior	120

Number of computers installed in various buildings are:

Buildings	Number of computers
Junior	40
Middle	40
Senior	100
Admin	20

(a) Suggest the suitable place to install the server. Justify your answer.

(b) Suggest the most suitable layout.

(c) Which device to be installed in each building to connect the computers within that building?

(d) Where to place the repeater?

(e) Suggest a device required to provide wireless internet access to all laptops and smartphones.

39. With reference to the above given tables in question number 36, write commands in SQL for the following: 5

(a) To display the name of the Patients, TestID and Test name for those patients who were admitted in the year 2020.

(b) To display the names of the patients, test names and cost of test they tested for.

(c) To display the names of all the patients who has COVID test.

(d) To increase cost by 5% of those tests in the TEST table which are below 100.

(e) Delete the record from Patient table with TESTID T05.

40. Consider a binary file employee.dat containing details such as empno: ename: salary (separator ':'). 5

(a) Write a python function to add employees details in the employee.dat.

(b) Write a python function to display the details of those employees who are earning between 2000 and 5000 (both values inclusive).

Solved Sample Paper – 5 (Theory) - Answers

PART – A

SECTION – I

1. (b) try (c) True

½ mark for each correct option

2. Invalid variable name:

(c) 4Area

A variable name must not start with a number.

½ mark for choosing the correct option
½ mark for valid reason

3. Output:

14

Ever

½ mark for each correct line of output

4. Roll_no – identifier

if – keyword

½ mark for each correct answer

5. (c) and

1 mark for correct answer

6. Dict={'301':'English', '041':'Mathematics','042':'Physics'}

1 mark for the correct statement

7. Output:

(9, 23)

½ mark for each correct number in the output

8. (a) math

(b) csv

½ mark for each correct module name

9. (a) VoIP (Voice Over Internet Protocol)

(b) IRC (Internet Relay Chat)

½ mark for each correct answer

10. Ransomware

1 mark for the correct answer

11. UPDATE

1 mark for the correct answer

12. In SQL, the NOT NULL constraint applied to a column enforces that column not to accept NULL (i.e. empty) values. This means that field will always have a value while inserting a new record.

1 mark for any correct answer

13. Desc keyword of Order By command is used to sort the records of a table in descending order.

1 mark for correct answer

14. (a) DELETE and (c) UPDATE

½ mark for each correct option

15. Optical Fibre

1 mark for the correct answer

16. Strings are sequences of characters. A string in python is declared by enclosing these characters in single quote / double quote.

Strings in python is a sequence of Unicode characters.

1 mark for any correct definition of string

17. Output:

['Learning', 'Python', 'is', 'fun']

1 mark for the correct output

18. A foreign key is an attribute in a relation which acts like a primary key in another relation. A foreign key is used to create a relation between two tables.

1 mark for any correct definition of foreign key

19. The main purpose of a cookie is to identify users and to save the login credentials. Cookies lets browser remember your login credentials, shopping carts and many more.

1 mark for any correct importance of cookies

20. DBMS (Database Management System) is a system that allows the users to store the data, define it, retrieve it and update the information.

1 mark for any correct use of DBMS

21. IP (Internet Protocol) address is a unique number associated with every computer in the computer network for identification of the computer.

1 mark for any correct definition of IP address

SECTION – II

22. (a) CREATE TABLE RESULT(ST_ID integer, NAME char(20),
EXAMID integer, MARKS integer);

1 mark for the correct statement

(b) SELECT DISTINCT (COUNT ST_ID) FROM RESULT;
SELECT COUNT(DISTINCT ST_ID) FROM RESULT;

1 mark for the correct statement

(c) CREATE TABLE STUDENT(ST_ID INTEGER PRIMARY KEY,
NAME CHAR(20), CLASS CHAR(5), SECTION CHAR(1));

1 mark for the correct statement

(d) ALTER TABLE STUDENT ADD(MOBILE CHAR(10));

(e) UPDATE RESULT SET NAME="Devansh" WHERE NAME="Devanh"

23.
```
import csv
import os
def Add_Book(L):
    with open("Book.csv",'a',newline='') as a:
        c=csv.writer(a)
        c.writerow(L)
def Display():
    with open("Book.csv",'r') as c:
        cw=csv.reader(c)
        for x in cw:
            print(x)
def DelSel(r):
    l=[]
    flag=0
    with open('Book.csv','r') as a:
        c=csv.reader(a)
        for x in c:
            l.append(x)
            if x[0]==str(r):
                l.remove(x)
                flag=1
    with open('temp.csv','w',newline='') as b:
        d=csv.writer(b)
        d.writerows(l)
    if flag==0:
        print("Not found")
    else:
        print(r, "deleted successfully")
    os.remove('Book.csv')
    os.rename('temp.csv','Book.csv')
L1=[1,"NCERT Maths 8",150]
L2=[2,"NCERT Science 8",180]
L3=[3,"NCERT Maths 9",180]
Add_Book(L1)
Add_Book(L2)
Add_Book(L3)
DelSel(3)
Display()
```

(a) os module

1 mark for the correct module name

(b) writer()

1 mark for the correct answer

(c) cw

1 mark for the correct answer

(d) remove()

1 mark for the correct answer.

(e) 3 deleted successfully
['1', 'NCERT Maths 8', '150']
['2', 'NCERT Science 8', '180']

1 mark for the correct output

PART – B

SECTION – I

24. (a) 14.75
(b) 27

1 mark for each correct output

25. (a) Assigning login and password to let authorise person login to the network.
(b) Installing firewall
(c) Assigning proper file permissions so that only people with proper rights can edit or delete.

1 mark for any correct point

26. (a) **NIC:** Network Interface Card
(b) **MAN:** Metropolitan Area Network
(c) **ISP:** Internet Service Provider
(d) **IP:** Internet Protocol

½ mark for each correct full form

27. Try..except block is used to catch and handle exceptions. The set of statements to be executed are placed in the try block and if any exceptions are going to be there then that is handled by except block. Otherwise exceptions interrupt the normal flow of the program.

```
def divide(x,y):
    try:
        print(x/y)
    except ZeroDivisionError:
        print("Cannot divide by 0")

divide(7,3)
divide(5,0)
```

1 mark for writing use of try..except block
1 mark for the example function

28.
```
A=20
for B in range(0, A):
    if B%3==0:
        print(B*3)
    else:
        print(B+3)
```

½ mark for each correction

29. Possible outputs:

(b) n-h-n-h

(c) n-o-n-t

Maximum value for x=5 and Minimum value for x=2

½ mark for each correct possible outcome
½ mark for each correct maximum and minimum value of x

30. (a) 150.0

(b) 300

1 mark for each correct output

31. Cursors are used by database programmers to process individual rows returned by database system queries. Cursors enable manipulation of whole result sets at once. In this scenario, a cursor enables the sequential processing of rows in a result set.

(a) Cursor.fetchone()

(c) Cursor.fetchall()

(e) Cursor.execute()

½ mark for each correct valid cursor method

32. DELETE FROM EMPLOYEE

WHERE EmpID = 201;

1 mark for first part of the query
1 mark for second part of the query

33. Output:

0

25

9

1

½ mark for each correct line of output

SECTION – II

34.
```
def arrange(A):
    j=0
    for i in range(0,len(A)):
        if A[i]<0:
            t=A[i]
            A[i]=A[j]
            A[j]=t
            j=j+1
    print(A)
```

½ mark for declaring j and initialising it to 0
½ mark using for loop to iterate on each element in the list
½ mark for checking the element
1 mark for swapping
½ mark for final display statement

35.
```
def show_caps():
    try:
        with open("notes.txt","r")as fin:
            ch=fin.read()
            print(ch.upper())
    except FileNotFoundError:
        print("File doesnot exist")
```

½ mark for try and except block
½ mark for opening the file in correct mode
1 mark for reading the contents of the file
1 mark for displaying all the contents in uppercase

36. (a)

TESTID
T01
T05
T03

(b)

TESTID	COUNT(*)
T01	1
T05	3
T03	1

(c) NAME

Suraj

Tina

Pratibha

1 mark for each correct output

37.
```
def PushOn(Book):
    N=input("Enter the Title of the book")
    Book.append(N)
    print(Book)

def PopOut(Book):
    if len(Book)==0:
        print("Empty List")
    else:
        print(Book.pop()," deleted successfully")
    print(Book)
```

½ mark for reading the title of the book
½ mark for adding to the end of the list Book
½ mark for showing the list Book
½ mark for checking the length of the Book
½ mark for deleting the last element and displaying
½ mark for displaying the final list Book

SECTION – III

38. (a) Senior building because of maximum number of computers in that building

½ mark for naming the building and ½ mark for justification

(b) Star Topology

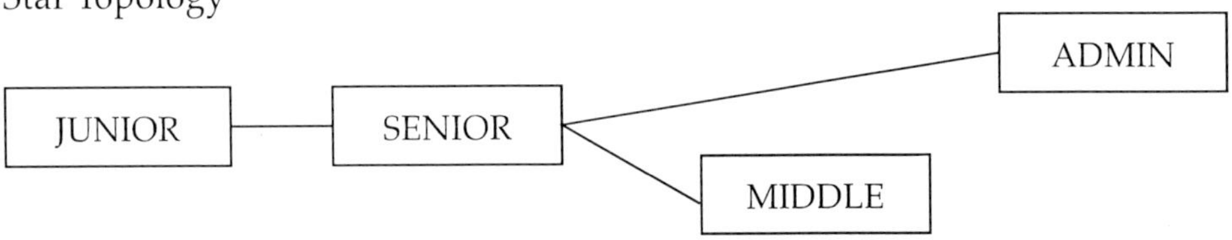

½ mark for topology and ½ mark for layout

(b) Hub/ Switch — 1 mark for the correct answer

(c) Repeater to be placed between Senior and Middle building

1 mark for the correct answer

(d) WiFi router or Router or Wireless modem — 1 mark for any correct answer

39. (a) SELECT NAME, P.TESTID, TESTNAME FROM PATIENT P, TEST T WHERE P.TESTID=T.TESTID AND YEAR(ADMISSION)=2020;

½ mark for 1st part of the statement
½ mark for 2nd part of the statement

(b) SELECT NAME, TESTNAME, COST FROM PATIENT P, TEST T
WHERE P.TESTID=T.TESTID;

½ mark for 1st part of the statement
½ mark for 2nd part of the statement

(c) SELECT NAME FROM PATIENT P, TEST T
P.TESTID=T.TESTID AND TESTNAME="COVID";

½ mark for 1st part of the statement
½ mark for 2nd part of the statement

(d) UPDATE TEST SET COST = COST + COST*5/100
WHERE COST<100;

½ mark for 1st part of the statement
½ mark for 2nd part of the statement

(e) DELETE FROM PATIENT WHERE TESTID='T05';

40.
```
import pickle
```
a)
```
def create():
    with open('employee.dat','ab') as fout:
        eno=input("Enter employee no")
        en=input("Enter employee name")
        sal=input("Enter salary")
        L=[eno, en, int(sal)]
        pickle.dump(L,fout)
```

b)
```
def display():
    with open('employee.dat','rb')as fin:
        while True:
            try:
                L=pickle.load(fin)
                if 2000<L[2]<5000:
                    print(L)

            except:
                break
```

½ mark for import pickle
½ mark for opening file in correct mode
½ mark for reading the contents
½ mark for making it in list
½ mark for dump method
½ mark for opening file in read mode
½ mark for while loop
½ mark for try and except block
½ mark for loading the record
½ mark for checking condition and display

Self-Assessment

Computer Science (083)

Self-Assessment Paper – 1 (Theory)

M.M.: 70 **Time: 3 hrs**

General Instructions

1. This question paper contains two parts A and B. Each part is compulsory.
2. Both Part A and Part B have choices.
3. Part-A has 2 sections:
   a. Section – I is short answer questions, to be answered in one word or one line.
   b. Section – II has two case studies questions. Each case study has 4 case-based subparts. An examinee is to attempt any 4 out of the 5 subparts.
4. Part - B is Descriptive Paper.
5. Part- B has three sections
   a. Section-I is short answer questions of 2 marks each in which two question have internal options.
   b. Section-II is long answer questions of 3 marks each in which two questions have internal options.
   c. Section-III is very long answer questions of 5 marks each in which one question has internal option.
6. All programming questions are to be answered using Python Language only.

PART – A

SECTION – I

Attempt any 15 questions from question numbers 1 to 21. Each question carries 1 mark. **(1 × 15 = 15 marks)**

1. Name any two keywords in Python that are not in lowercase. 1

2. Write the output of the following code segment: 1

```
Languages = ["Hindi", "English", "Bengali", "Punjabi", "French"]
print(Languages[ -3 : -1 : 1 ])
```

3. Which of the following command is used to open a file "c:\story.txt" in read-mode only? 1

(a) F = open("C:\story.txt", "r") (b) F = open("C:\story.txt", "a")

(c) F = open("C:\story.txt", "w") (d) F = open("C:\story.txt", "r+")

4. Write the name of the built-in function/ method to perform the following task: 1

(a) To calculate the middle element of data i.e. median.

(b) To return the absolute value of the number.

5. How are operators with equal priority evaluated in an expression? 1

6. Write the use of slicing in Python with an example. 1

7. Define tuple in Python. 1

8. Name the Python Library modules which need to be imported to invoke the following functions: 1

(a) mean (b) factorial

9. Name the protocol to transfer files, videos, images over the world wide web. 1

10. Define Cybersecurity. 1

11. Define relation in SQL. 1

12. Name the list matching operator in SQL. 1

13. Which SQL function is used to display the day of the week (i.e. Sunday, Monday, Tuesday,...) from specified date? 1

14. Write any one difference between IN and BETWEEN operators. 1

15. Which feature of many internet browsers allow users to access web pages without any information (like browsing history) being stored by the browser? 1

16. Write any one difference between pass and break statement in Python. 1

17. Give the output of the following code: 1

Str1="Python is an interpreted progamming language"

print(Str1.split())

18. Write any two relational operators in SQL. 1

19. Define OSS. 1

20. What is the purpose of SQL? 1

21. What is the basic difference between virus and worm? 1

SECTION – II

Consists of case study questions and are compulsory to attempt. Attempt any 4 sub parts from each question. Each sub part carries 1 mark. (4 + 4 = 8 marks)

22. Aryan is a database manager. He has been approached by a music library store to maintain the inventory for his store to store the following details using SQL:

- Name of the database – Library
- Name of the table – Music
- The attributes / fields of Music relation are:

  Code – character of size 3 (contains unique values)

  Title – character of size 25 (Not Null constraint)

  Type – character of size 20 (can accept null values)

  Rating – numeric value of type integer (default value as 1)

Table: MUSIC				
Code	**Title**	**Singers**	**Type**	**Rating**
M001	Lagdi Lahore Di Aa	Guru Randhawa	Romantic	3
M002	Nagada Sang Dhol Baaje	Shreya Ghoshal	Dance	5
M003	Bada Pachtaoge	Arijit Singh	NULL	4
M004	O Saki Saki	Neha Kakkar	Dance	5
M005	Ik Vaari Aa	Arijit Singh	Romantic	4

(a) Identify the candidate keys and most appropriate primary key. 1

(b) Write a DDL statement to create the table Music with appropriate constraints applied. 1

(c) Write a DML statement to insert the following record in the table Music: Code='M006', Title='Tera Ban Jaunga', Type='Romantic', Rating=3 1

(d) Write s SQL statement to display all the records where Type is having value NULL. 1

(e) Write the output of the following statement: 1

SELECT COUNT(Type) FROM MUSIC;

23. Aryan is writing a Python program for creating a csv file "SongList.csv" to store the details of SNo, Title of the song and star rating. He has written the following code and getting some of the errors and not able to fill in the blanks. Help him to solve his problem.

```
import csv

def Add_Song(L):
    with open("SongList.csv",'a',newline='') as a:
        c=csv.writer(a)
        c.writerow(L)
def Disp_Songs():
    with open("SongList.csv",'r') as c:
        cw=csv.reader(c)
        for x in cw:
            print(x)
```

```
def Update(id, R):
    l=[]
    flag=0
    a=open('SongList.csv','r')
    b=open('temp.csv','_', newline='')        #Line 1
    c=csv.reader(a)
    for x in c:
        if x[0]==str(id):
            x[2]=R
            flag=1
        d=csv.writer(b)
        d.writerow(x)
    if flag==0:
        print("Not found")
    else:
        print("Updated successfully")
    a.close()
    b.close()
    os.________('SongList.csv')                #Line 2
    os.________('temp.csv','SongList.csv')    #Line 3
L1=[1,"Nagada",4]
L2=[2,"O Saki Saki",5]
L3=[3,"Mahi Ve",3]
Add_Song(L1)
Add_Song(L2)
Add_Song(L3)
Update(3, 4)
Disp_Songs()
```

(a) Help Aryan to rectify the following error while executing the code:
NameError: name 'os' is not defined 1

(b) Write the correct file mode in fill in the blank for Line 1. 1

(c) Fill in the blank for Line 2 to delete the csv file. 1

(d) Fill in the blank for Line 4 to change the name of the files. 1

(e) Write the output of the program while executing the code. 1

PART – B

SECTION – I

Each question carries 2 marks **(2 × 10 = 20)**

24. Evaluate the following expressions: 2

(a) 2*3**3*4 (b) 2%6

25. Differentiate between Star Topology and Bus Topology. 2

26. Write the full form of the following: 2

(a) CDMA (b) MBPS (c) WAN (d) URI

27. Write any four advantages of using functions. 2

OR

Write a user defined function Power(X,N) in Python to return the result of X raised to the power N where X and N are non-negative integers.

For example, if X is 5 and N is 3 then the function should return the result of (5)3 is 125.

28. Rewrite the following code in Python after removing all syntax error(s). Underline each correction done in the code. 2

```
A=20
WHILE A<=50
if A>=30
    print(A)
    A=A+10
ELSE:
    print(A*2)
    A+=3
```

29. What possible output(s) are expected to be displayed on screen at the time of execution of the program from the following code? Also specify the minimum values that can be assigned to each of the variables B and L. 2

```
import random
values = [10, 20, 30, 40, 50, 60, 70, 80]
B=random.randint(3,5)
L=random.randint(B,7)

for I in range(B, L):
    print(values[I], end='-')
```

(i) 10-20- (ii) 40- (iii) 20-30-40- (iv) 40-50-60-

30. Name SQL functions for each of the following that: 2

(a) Returns a number

(b) Returns lowercase letters

(c) Returns names of days (i.e. Monday, Tuesday, etc)

(d) Returns weekday number (i.e. 1 for Sunday, 2 for Monday and so on)

31. Ruhi has written the Python code to create the table Teacher (TID, Tname) and display the structure of the table of SCHOOL database in SQL. She is getting few errors in the code and left those places as blank. Help her to fill the blanks to execute the code successfully. 2

```
mydb=mysql.connector.connect(host="localhost",user="root",
                             passwd="root",database="school")
mycursor=mydb.cursor()
s="______________Teacher(TID varchar(2), TName varchar(20))"    #Line 1
mycursor.________(s)                                             #Line 2
print("Table created successfully")
mycursor.execute("_____Teacher")                                 #Line 3
for x in mycursor:
      print(x)
```

(a) Help Ruhi to solve the following error: NameError: name 'mysql' is not defined.

(b) Fill in the blank in Line 1 to complete the SQL statement to create the structure of the table.

(c) Write the method to run the query by fill the blank in line 2.

(d) Fill in the blank in Line 3 to display the structure of the table.

32. Define Cartesian Product with the help of an example. 2

33. Find and write the output of the following python code: 2

```
def Update(M1, M2, M3):
    for I in range(0, len(M1)):
        if M1[I]>='A' and M1[I]<='N':
            M3+=M1[I]
        elif M1[I]>='M' and M1[I]<='Z':
            M3+=M2[I]
        else:
            M3+='$'
    return M3


M1="PYTHON"
M2="Programming"
M3=""
print(Update(M1, M2, M3))
```

SECTION – II

Each question carries 3 marks **(3 × 4 = 12)**

34. Write a user defined function Count37(N) in Python to find and display the count of all those numbers and sum of those numbers which are between 1 and N, which are either divisible by 3 or by 7. 3

For example: If the value of N is 15

The count of numbers between 1 and 15: 7

The sum of numbers divisible by 3 or 7 between 1 and 15: 66

(*Note:* N is 15 and numbers between 1 to 15 which are either divisible by 3 or 7 are 3, 6, 7, 9, 12, 14, 15 and the count is 7)

35. Write a user defined function DisplayP() in Python to read lines from a text file "diary.txt, display and count the number of lines starting with I. 3

For example, the contents of diary.txt is:

I love programming with Python.

It is fun to work with different modules in Python.

Python is used for various purposes.

The output of the function is:

I love progamming with Python.

It is fun to work with different modules in Python.

Total number of lines starting with I : 2

36. Write output for the following SQL queries (a) to (c) based on the relations COMPANY and CUSTOMER given below: 3

Table: COMPANY

ID	CNAME	CITY	PNAME
1	OPPO	NEW DELHI	MOBILE
2	APPLE	MUMBAI	MOBILE
3	SONY	UTTAR PRADESH	TV
4	BLACKBERRY	MUMBAI	MOBILE
5	SAMSUNG	UTTAR PRADESH	TV

Table: CUSTOMER

CID	Name	PRICE	QTY	ID
1	Sarita	75000	2	1
2	Shalini	75000	4	2
3	Annu	56000	10	3
4	Balwinder	45000	5	1

(a) SELECT COUNT(*), CITY FROM COMPANY GROUP BY CITY

(b) SELECT MIN(PRICE), MAX(PRICE) FROM CUSTOMER WHERE QTY>=5;

(c) SELECT ID, AVG(PRICE) FROM CUSTOMER GROUP BY ID;

37. Evaluate the following postfix expression. Show the status of stack after execution of each operation separately: 3

2, 13, +, 5, -, 6, 3, /, 5, *, <

OR

Write a user defined function PushN(L, X) in Python to add number X to the end of the list L and a user defined function PopN() which is invoked to remove the last element from the list L considering it to act as insert and delete operation of the stack data structure.

SECTION – III

Each question carries 5 marks **(5 × 3 = 15)**

38. Techwin Solution Ltd. has set up its new centre in Mumbai. It has four buildings as shown in the diagram given below: 5

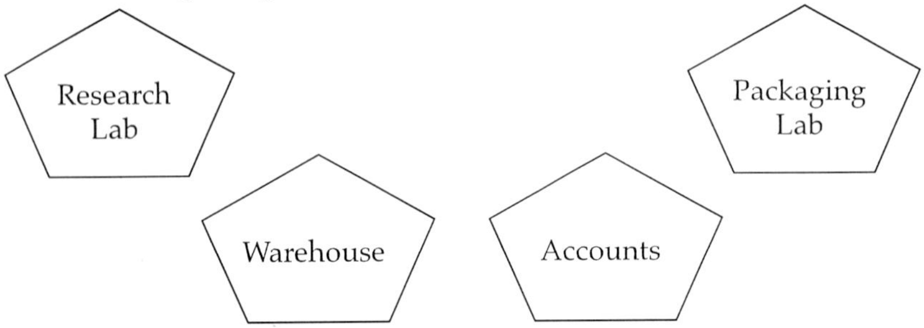

Distance between various buildings are:

Accounts to Research Lab	100 m
Accounts to Warehouse	60 m
Warehouse to Packaging Unit	160 m
Packaging Unit to Research Lab	150 m
Accounts to Packaging Lab	50 m
Warehouse to Research Lab	60 m

Number of computers:

Accounts	10
Research Lab	100
Packaging Unit	50
Warehouse	20

As a network expert, provide the best possible answer for the following queries:

(a) Suggest the most suitable cable layout for connecting various buildings.

(b) Suggest the most suitable place to house the serve of this organisation.

(c) Which device is placed in each building to connect the computers within the building?

(d) Suggest the placement of repeater with justification.

(e) Suggest a system (hardware / software) to prevent unauthorized access to or from the network.

39. Write SQL commands for the following queries (a) to (e) based on the relations COMPANY and CUSTOMER given in Question Number 36: 5

(a) To display those company name which are having price more than 70000.

(b) To display the report having CID, Name, CName, Amount from Table Customer and Company. Amount is to be calculated as the product of QTY and PRICE.

(c) To increase the price by 5% for those customer whose name has 'a' in it.

(d) To add one more column GST to the table Customer having numeric values with decimal values to two places.

(e) To calculate and insert the GST as 5% of the amount to be paid. Amount is the product of Price * Qty.

40. The student record contains rollno, name and score in the form of a dictionary object. 5

(a) Write a user defined function writeinto() in Python to read a record in the form of a dictionary and write it into student.dat

(b) Write a user defined function readfrom() in Python to read all the records from student.dat in dictionary format and display.

Self-Assessment Paper – 2 (Theory)

M.M.: 70 **Time: 3 hrs**

General Instructions

1. This question paper contains two parts A and B. Each part is compulsory.
2. Both Part A and Part B have choices.
3. Part-A has 2 sections:
   a. Section – I is short answer questions, to be answered in one word or one line.
   b. Section – II has two case studies questions. Each case study has 4 case-based subparts. An examinee is to attempt any 4 out of the 5 subparts.
4. Part - B is Descriptive Paper.
5. Part- B has three sections
   a. Section-I is short answer questions of 2 marks each in which two question have internal options.
   b. Section-II is long answer questions of 3 marks each in which two questions have internal options.
   c. Section-III is very long answer questions of 5 marks each in which one question has internal option.
6. All programming questions are to be answered using Python Language only.

PART – A

SECTION – I

Attempt any 15 questions from question numbers 1 to 21. Each question carries 1 mark. **(1 × 15 = 15 marks)**

1. Write any two rules for creating an identifier in Python. 1

2. Write the output of the following code segment: 1

Languages = ["Hindi", "English", "Bengali", "Punjabi", "French"]

print(Languages[-1 : -3 : -1])

3. Which of the following command is used to open a file "c:\story.txt" in write-mode only? 1

(a) F = open("C:\story.txt", "r") (b) F = open("C:\story.txt", "a")

(c) F = open("C:\story.txt", "w") (d) F = open("C:\story.txt", "r+")

4. Write the name of the built-in function/ method to perform the following task: 1

(a) Convert the first character to upper case.

(b) To calculate the exponential value.

5. Which operator is used for floor division? 1

6. What is the use of index in Python? 1

7. What is the use of return keyword in Python? 1

8. Name the Python Library modules which need to be imported to invoke the following functions: 1

   (a) fabs() (b) writerows()

9. Name the client server protocol which holds the email for receiving emails. 1

10. What is IPR? 1

11. Which operator in SQL is known as pattern matching operator? 1

12. What is the use of default constraint in SQL? 1

13. Write the SQL statement to display the month name from the current system date. 1

14. What is the purpose of group functions in SQL? Name any one such function. 1

15. What does the "https://" at the beginning of a URL denote? 1

16. Write any one difference between for and while loop. 1

17. Give the output of the following code: 1

```
Str1="DIFFERENCE"
Print(Str1.find("E"))
```

18. Define Candidate key with the help of an example. 1

19. Name any two web browsers. 1

20. Write the SQL statement to display all the names of the databases. 1

21. Categorise the following under Client side and server-side scripting languages: 1

   (a) ASP (b) JavaScript (c) VBScript (d) JSP

SECTION – II

Consists of case study questions and are compulsory to attempt. Attempt any 4 sub parts from each question. Each sub part carries 1 mark. (4 + 4 = 8 marks)

22. Mukesh is a database manager. He has been approached by a Sports store to maintain the inventory for his store having the following details using SQL:

   - Name of the database – Store
   - Name of the table – Sports
   - The attributes / fields of Sports relation are:

Code – character of size 3 (contains unique values)

Item – character of size 25 (Not Null constraint)

Qty – numeric value of type integer (can accept null values)

Price – numeric value of type integer (default value as 50)

Code	Item	Qty	Price
S001	Skipping Rope	100	50
F002	Football – 3	200	200
B003	Badminton	120	450
S004	Sipper	NULL	1050
F005	Football – 5	110	2050

(a) Identify the primary key and mention the reason for choosing primary key. 1

(b) Write a DDL statement to create a database STORE and then write a statement to make use of this database. 1

(c) Write a DDL statement to create the table Sports with appropriate constraint. 1

(d) Write a DML statement to insert a record with some valid values. 1

(e) Write a DML statement to count the number of records having values in the quantity field. 1

23. Mukesh is writing a Python program for creating a csv file "Sports.csv" to store the details of SNo, Item name, Quantity and Price. He has written the following code and getting some of the errors and not able to fill in the blanks. Help him to solve his problem.

```
import csv

def Add_Item():
    with open("Sports.csv",'a',____________) as a:    #Line 1
        c=csv.________(a)                              #Line 2
        i=1
        item="Football"
        qty=4
        price=400
        T=[i, item, qty, price]
        c.writerow(T)
def Disp_items():
    with open("Sports.csv",'r') as c:
        cw=csv.________(c)                             #Line 3
        for x in cw:
            print(x)

Add_Item()
____________                                           #Line 4
```

(a) Fill in the blank for Line 1. 1

(b) Fill in the blank for Line 2 to create the writer object. 1

(c) Fill in the blank for Line 3 for reading from csv file. 1

(d) Fill in the blank for Line 4 by invoking the function for displaying all the items. 1

(e) Write the output of the program when executed. 1

PART – B

SECTION – I

Each question carries 2 marks **(2 × 10 = 20)**

24. Evaluate the following expressions: 2

(a) 10**2>100 and 50<100 (b) 2**3**2

25. Define Firewall. 2

26. Write the full forms of the following: 2

(a) URL (b) SSH (c) UTF (d) ISCII

27. Write a user defined function IsPrime(N) in Python to check if the parameter N is a prime number or not. The function should return True if the number is prime otherwise return False. 2

28. Rewrite the following code in Python after removing all syntax error(s). Underline each correction done in the code. 2

```
def Total(N)
    sum=0
    for C in Range(1, N+1):
        sum+=C
    RETURN sum
print(Sum(2))
print(Tot(5))
```

29. What possible output(s) are expected to be displayed on screen at the time of execution of the program from the following code? Also specify the minimum and maximum values that can be assigned to the variable X. 2

```
import random
STRING="PYTHON PROGRAM"
X=random.randint(0,3)
Y=13
while STRING[Y]!='G':
    print(STRING[Y]+STRING[X], end="$")
    X=X+1
    Y=Y-1
```

(i) MPAYRT$ (ii) PYMYAT$ (iii) MAGRAY$ (iv) MYATRH$

30. Name SQL functions for each of the following that: 2

(a) Returns absolute value of a number

(b) Check if the letters in the string is in lowercase letters

(c) Returns day from the system date

(d) Returns all letters in uppercase

31. Kapil has written the Python code to create the table STUDENT(ANO, NAME) and display the structure of the table of SCHOOL database in SQL. He is getting few errors in the code and left those places as blank. Help him to fill up the blanks to execute the code successfully. 2

```
import mysql.connector
mydb=mysql.connector.connect(host="__________",user="root",     #Line 1
                    passwd="root",database="school")
mycursor=mydb.________        #Line 2
s="Create table STUDENT(ANO varchar(2), Name varchar(20))"
__________.execute(s)     #Line3
print("Table created successfully")
mycursor.________("DESC STUDENT")        #Line 4
for x in mycursor:
      print(x)
```

(a) Fill in the blank in Line 1

(b) Fill in the blank in Line 2

(c) Fill in the blank in Line 3

(d) Fill in the blank in Line 4

32. Define Union operation in context of a relational database with the help of an example. 2

33. Find and write the output of the following Python code: 2

```
for Name in ['Annu','Kavita','Jaya','Balwinder','Pratibha']:
    print(Name)
    if Name[0]=='J':
        break
else:
    print('Finished')
print('Got it')
```

SECTION – II

Each question carries 3 marks **(3 × 4 = 12)**

34. Write a user defined function SumNat(N) in Python to return the sum of the first N natural numbers. 3

For example, if N is 10 then the function should return (1 + 2 + 3 + ... + 10 = 55).

35. Write a user defined function count() in Python to count the number of lines present in the text file "diary.txt". 3

36. Write output for the following SQL queries (a) to (c) based on the relations ACCOUNT and TRANACT given below: 3

Table: ACCOUNT		
ANO	**ANAME**	**CITY**
1	RAKHEE	NEW DELHI
2	SAKSHI	MUMBAI
3	SARITA	UTTAR PRADESH
4	MEENAKSHI	MUMBAI
5	JAYA	UTTAR PRADESH

Table: TRANSACT				
TID	**ANO**	**TYPE**	**AMOUNT**	**DOT**
1	1	W	1500	2020-09-21
2	2	D	5000	2020-09-21
3	1	D	2000	2020-10-20
4	1	D	1000	2020-10-22

(a) SELECT ANO, ANAME FROM ACCOUNT WHERE CITY NOT IN 'MUMBAI';

(b) SELECT DISTINCT ANO FROM TRANSACT;

(c) SELECT TYPE, SUM(AMOUNT), COUNT(*) FROM TRANSACT GROUP BY TYPE HAVING TYPE='D';

37. Write PUSH(ACCOUTS) and POP(ACCOUNTS) methods in Python to add Account and remove Account considering them to act as Push and Pop operations of Stack. 3

Note: Account will include the details of AccountNo, Name, TypeAcc

SECTION – III

Each question carries 5 marks **(5 × 3 = 15)**

38. Ambiance is an educational organisation. It is planning to setup its branch in the same city with its head office in Safdarjung Enclave. The Green Park branch has 4 buildings – ADMIN, JUNIOR, MIDDLE and SENIOR. 5

You as a network expert have to suggest the best network related solutions for their problems raised in (a) to (e), keeping in mind the distances between the buildings and other given parameters.

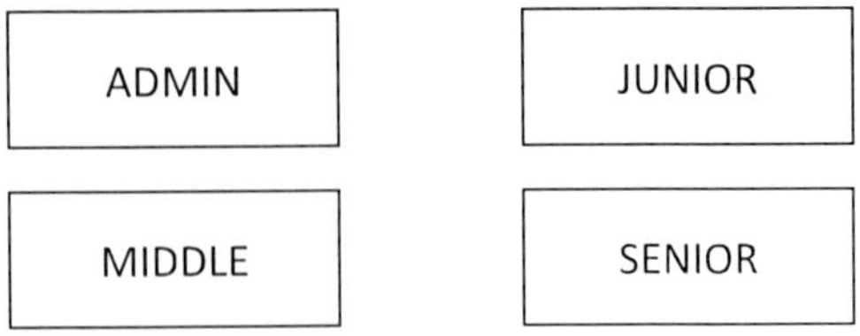

Distance between various buildings:

ADMIN TO JUNIOR	50 m
JUNIOR TO MIDDLE	75 m
MIDDLE TO SENIOR	65 m
SENIOR TO ADMIN	70 m
SENIOR TO JUNIOR	30 m

Number of computers installed at various buildings are:

ADMIN	20
JUNIOR	70
MIDDLE	80
SENIOR	100

(a) Suggest the most suitable place to house the server with justification.

(b) Draw the cable layout to join the buildings and name the topology.

(c) Which hardware device is required to connect the computers within the same building?

(d) Suggest the placement of repeater (if any).

(e) Which one of the following will you suggest to establish the online face-to-face communication between the people of Admin Office in Green Park branch and Safdarjung Head Office.

39. Write SQL commands for the following queries (a) to (e) based on the relations ACCOUNT and TRANSACT: 5

Table: ACCOUNT		
ANO	**ANAME**	**CITY**
1	RAKHEE	NEW DELHI
2	SAKSHI	MUMBAI
3	SARITA	UTTAR PRADESH
4	MEENAKSHI	MUMBAI
5	JAYA	UTTAR PRADESH

Table: TRANSACT				
TID	ANO	TYPE	AMOUNT	DOT
1	1	W	1500	2020-09-21
2	2	D	5000	2020-09-21
3	1	D	2000	2020-10-20
4	1	D	1000	2020-10-22

(a) To display the details of transactions of Type Deposit from table TRANSACT.

(b) To display ANO and Amount of all Deposits and withdrawals in the month of October from the table.

(c) To display the last date of transaction from the table TRANSACT for the accounts having ANO as 1.

(d) To display the ANO, ANAME from table TRANSACT and ACCOUNT.

(e) To display the total number of records TYPE wise from TRANSACT table.

40. The employee record contains employee code, name and salary. It should be stored in a list object. 5

(a) Write a user defined function in Python to read values from user for a record and add it to the binary file "emp.dat"

(b) Write a user defined function Search(N) in Python which takes N as a parameter for Name of the employee, search and display the record.

Self-Assessment Paper – 3 (Theory)

M.M.: 70 **Time: 3 hrs**

General Instructions

1. This question paper contains two parts A and B. Each part is compulsory.
2. Both Part A and Part B have choices.
3. Part-A has 2 sections:
   a. Section – I is short answer questions, to be answered in one word or one line.
   b. Section – II has two case studies questions. Each case study has 4 case-based subparts. An examinee is to attempt any 4 out of the 5 subparts.
4. Part - B is Descriptive Paper.
5. Part- B has three sections
   a. Section-I is short answer questions of 2 marks each in which two question have internal options.
   b. Section-II is long answer questions of 3 marks each in which two questions have internal options.
   c. Section-III is very long answer questions of 5 marks each in which one question has internal option.
6. All programming questions are to be answered using Python Language only.

PART – A

SECTION – I

Attempt any 15 questions from question numbers 1 to 21. Each question carries 1 mark. **(1 × 15 = 15 marks)**

1. What is the use of keyword in Python? 1

2. Write the output of the following code segment: 1

Nos = (1, 5, 7, 3, 9, 11, 4, 6)

print(sum(Nos)/len(Nos))

3. Which of the following command is used to open a file "c:\story.txt" in append-mode? 1

(a) F = open("C:\story.txt", "r") (b) F = open("C:\story.txt", "a")

(c) F = open("C:\story.txt", "w") (d) F = open("C:\story.txt", "r+")

4. Write the name of the built-in function/ method to perform the following task: 1

(a) Returns the number of times a specified value occurs in a string.

(b) Searches the string for a specified value and returns the position of the value.

5. Write the difference between = and == operators. 1

6. Define function in Python. 1

7. What is the purpose of id() function in Python? 1

8. Name the Python Library modules which need to be imported to invoke the following functions: 1

   (a) exp() (b) uniform()

9. Which protocol is used to create a simple link between two peers in a network to transport packets? 1

10. Define plagiarism. 1

11. What is the use of Unique constraint in SQL? 1

12. Name range matching operator in SQL. 1

13. Write a SQL statement to display the first character from Name field from Employee table. 1

14. How can you eliminate duplicate rows from a query result? 1

15. What is Trojan Horse? 1

16. Write any one difference between parameter and argument in Python. 1

17. Give the output of the following code: 1

```
Str1="Difference"
print(Str1.split('e'))
```

18. Name any two datatypes in SQL. 1

19. Write any two characteristics of Web 2.0. 1

20. Write SQL command to remove the content of the table along with its structure. 1

21. What is the basic difference between Trojan Horse and Computer Worm? 1

SECTION – II

Consists of case study questions and are compulsory to attempt. Attempt any 4 sub parts from each question. Each sub part carries 1 mark. (4 + 4 = 8 marks)

22. Ambareesh is a database manager. He has been approached by a Electronic item store to maintain the inventory for his store having the following details using SQL:

    - Name of the database – Store
    - Name of the table – Electronics

- The attributes / fields of Sports relation are:
  Code – character of size 3 (contains unique values)
  Item – character of size 25 (Not Null constraint)
  Qty – numeric value of type integer (can accept null values)
  Price – numeric value of type integer (default value as 50)

Code	Item	Brand	Qty	Price
L001	Laptop	HP	100	50000
R001	Refrigerator	Samsung	200	25000
L002	Laptop	Sony	120	45000
R002	Refrigerator	Godrej	NULL	10500
R003	Refrigerator	Whirlpool	110	20500

(a) Identify the primary key and mention the reason for choosing primary key. 1

(b) Write a DDL statement to create a database STORE and then write a statement to make use of this database. 1

(c) Write a DDL statement to create the table Electronics with appropriate constraint. 1

(d) Write a DML statement to insert a record with some valid values. 1

(e) Write a DML statement to count the number of records having values in the quantity field. 1

23. Sanchita is writing a Python code to create a csv file to store the players of football team in football.csv. She has written the code and getting some errors. So, she made those blanks. Help her to fill in those blanks to successfully run the code.

```
import csv

def Add_Sport(L1):
    a=open("Football.csv",'a',newline='')
    c=csv.writer(a)
    c.writerow(L1)
    ____________            #Line 1

def Disp_Sports():
    b=open("Football.csv",'r')
    cw=____________(b)    #Line 2
    for x in cw:
        ____________        #Line 3
    b.close()
```

```
P1=[1,"Devansh"]
P2=[2,"Priyanshu"]
Add_Sport(__)          #Line 4
Add_Sport(P2)
Disp_Sports()
```

(a) Fill in the blank for Line 1 to close the file.

(b) Write the statement in Line 2 to create the reader object

(c) Write the statement in Line 3 to display the record

(d) Write the proper argument in Line 4

(e) Write the output of the code.

PART – B

SECTION – I

Each question carries 2 marks **(2 × 10 = 20)**

24. Evaluate the following expressions: 2

(a) 1+2**3*4 (b) 10+2 > 20 and 10 < 12

25. Define Cracker. 2

26. Write the full form of the following: 2

(a) ASCII (b) GPL (c) CSV (d) PAN

27. Write a user defined function NoElements(ItemList, Value) to count and display the number of times the Value is present in the ItemList. 2

For example:

If the ItemList contains [12, 4, 9, 3, 12, 98, 29, 12] and Value contain 12

The function should display

12 found 3 times in the list

28. Rewrite the following code in Python after removing all syntax error(s). Underline each correction done in the code. 2

```
def chksum:
    x=input("Enter a number")
    if x%2=0:
        for i in range(2*x):
            print(i)
        loop else:
            print('#')

chksum()
```

29. What possible output(s) are expected to be displayed on screen at the time of execution of the program from the following code? Also specify the minimum and maximum values that can be assigned to the variable N. 2

```
import random
X=3
N=random.randint(1, X)
for i in range(N):
    print(i,'@',i+1)
```

(i) 1@2@ (ii) 1@2@ (iii) 0@1@ (iv) 0@1@
1@2@
2@3@

30. Write the output of the following SQL queries: 2

(a) SELECT SUBSTR('CBSE EXAMINATION', 6, 4);

(b) SELECT DAYNAME(DATE(SYSDATE()));

31. Balwinder has the created a table STUDENT in the SCHOOL database with the following data: 2

ROLLNO	NAME
1	ASHISH
2	CHARVI
12	AASTHA

She has entered wrong value for the ROLLNO for AASTHA. She has written the Python code to make changes in the ROLLNO as 3 instead of 12 and getting few errors in the code and left those places as blank. Help her to fill the blanks to execute the code successfully.

```
import mysql.connector
mydb=mysql.connector.connect(host="localhost",user="root",
                             passwd="root",database="SCHOOL")
mycursor=mydb.________()                          #Line 1
s="UPDATE STUDENT SET__________ WHERE NAME='AASTHA'"    #Line 2
mycursor.________(s)                              #Line 3
mydb.commit()
print("Updated successfully")
mycursor.execute("____________________")          #Line 4
res=mycursor.fetchall()
for x in res:
      print(x)
```

(a) Fill in the blank in Line 1 to create an instance of an object for creating a cursor.

(b) Fill in the blank in Line 2 to make the changes as required.

(c) Fill in the blank in Line 3 to run the SQL statement s.

(d) Fill in the blank in Line 4 to write the SQL statement to display all the records from Student table.

32. Write the use of RDBMS Projection operation with the help of an example. 2

33. Find and write the output of the following Python code: 2

```
def output():
    p='CBSE EXAM'
    i=0
    while p[i]!='A':
        print(p[i],end='@')
        i+=1
    print(i)

output()
```

SECTION – II

Each question carries 3 marks **(3 × 4 = 12)**

34. Write a user defined function NotMul(L, N) in Python which should display the value of all such elements and their corresponding locations in the List which are not multiples of 2 or 3. L is the list and N is the number of elements in the list. 3

For example, if the list contains

L=[3, 4, 13, 1, 2, 9, 11]

Then the function should display the following as an output:

13 at location 2

1 at location 3

11 at location 6

35. Write a user defined function WordCtr() in Python to read the text file "story.txt", count and display the total number words present in the file. 3

36. Consider the table 'Teacher' with the data given below and then give the output of the queries from (a) to (c) on the basis of the given table: 3

TID	NAME	DEPARTMENT	PERIODS
T101	Seema	Maths	24
T102	Bhanupriya	English	30
T103	Mohan	Maths	32
T104	Disha	English	30
T105	Prabhjot	English	NULL

(a) SELECT COUNT(DISTINCT DEPARTMENT) FROM TEACHER;

(b) SELECT DEPARTMENT, COUNT(*) FROM TEACHER GROUP BY DEPARTMENT;

(c) SELECT AVG(PERIODS), DEPARTMENT FROM TEACHER GROUP BY DEPARTMENT;

37. Write PUSH(Teacher) and POP(Teacher) methods in Python to add Teacher and remove Teacher considering them to act as Push and Pop operations of Stack.

Note: Teacher will include the details of TID, Name, Subject 3

SECTION – III

Each question carries 5 marks **(5 × 3 = 15)**

38. 'ABC Toys' is a small company manufacturing toys. Now, they are opening various branches (SALES, MANUFACTURING, WAREHOUSE, ADMIN) for as per the purpose of work within the same city to expand their business. 5

You as an administrator have to suggest the solutions for (a) to (e), keeping in mind the distances between the branches and other given parameters.

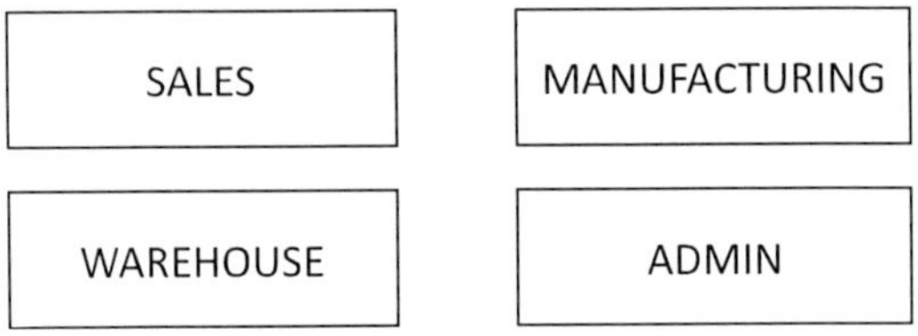

Distance between various branches (in metres):

Sales to Manufacturing	50
Manufacturing to Warehouse	100
Warehouse to Admin	60
Admin to Sales	90
Admin to Manufacturing	65

Number of computers installed in various branches are:

SALES	10
MANUFACTURING	2
WAREHOUSE	2
ADMIN	20

(a) Suggest the most suitable place to house the server with justification.

(b) Draw the cable layout to join the various branches and name the topology.

(c) Suggest the placement of repeater.

(d) Which device is required to be installed in all the branches so as to connect computers within it?

(e) They have also decided to create a website which would allow customers to order toys online. State how company would benefit from the website.

39. Write SQL commands for the following queries (a) to (e) based on the relations WATCH and SALE given below: 5

Table: WATCH

ID	NAME	TYPE	PRICE	QTY_STOCK
W1	GMT-Master II	Ladies	120000	100
W2	High Time	Ladies	50000	140
W3	Wave	Gents	12000	125
W4	High Fashion	Unisex	25000	220
W5	Golden Time	Gents	15000	100

Table: SALE

ID	QTY_SOLD	D_Sale
W1	1500	2020-09-21
W2	5000	2020-09-21
W3	2000	2020-10-20
W4	1000	2020-10-22

(a) To display the details of watches where the name ends with Time from WATCH table.

(b) To display the name of those watches where the price is in the range of 10000 to 20000 (inclusive of both the lower and upper limit) from WATCH table.

(c) To display Type and Total quantity in store.

(d) To display the ID, Qty_Sold and Amount from table SALE and WATCH. Amount is to be calculated as product of QTY_SOLD and PRICE.

(e) To display the details of all the watches in ascending order of their names.

40. Write a user defined functions in Python to perform the following operations on a binary file named "teacher.dat". The binary file stores the records of teachers with the following information of TID, Name and Department. 5

(a) To read the values for a record and add it into the binary file.

(b) To read the TID to delete that particular record.

Self-Assessment Paper – 4 (Theory)

M.M.: 70 **Time: 3 hrs**

General Instructions

1. This question paper contains two parts A and B. Each part is compulsory.
2. Both Part A and Part B have choices.
3. Part-A has 2 sections:
   a. Section – I is short answer questions, to be answered in one word or one line.
   b. Section – II has two case studies questions. Each case study has 4 case-based subparts. An examinee is to attempt any 4 out of the 5 subparts.
4. Part - B is Descriptive Paper.
5. Part- B has three sections
   a. Section-I is short answer questions of 2 marks each in which two question have internal options.
   b. Section-II is long answer questions of 3 marks each in which two questions have internal options.
   c. Section-III is very long answer questions of 5 marks each in which one question has internal option.
6. All programming questions are to be answered using Python Language only.

PART – A

SECTION – I

Attempt any 15 questions from question numbers 1 to 21. Each question carries 1 mark. **(1 × 15 = 15 marks)**

1. What is the use of type function/method in Python? 1

2. Write the output of the following code segment: 1

Languages = ["Hindi", "English", "Bengali", "Punjabi", "French"]

print(Languages[: : -1])

3. Which of the following command(s) can be used to read "5" characters from a file "story.txt" using the file object fin? 1

(a) fin.read() (b) fin.read(5) (c) fin.readline(5) (d) fin.readlines()

4. Write the name of the built-in function/ method to perform the following task: 1

(a) Returns true if all the characters in the string are lower case or not.

(b) Returns True if all characters in the string are digits.

5. Write any two comparison operators in Python. 1

6. Name the two different categories of functions. 1

7. When do you use the split() function in Python? 1

8. Name the Python Library modules which need to be imported to invoke the following functions: 1

   (a) floor() (b) remove()

9. Which protocol is a suite of communication protocol? 1

10. What is Cryptography? 1

11. Name any two single row functions (i.e. Scalar functions). 1

12. Differentiate between having and where clause. 1

13. Write SQL statement to display Name in uppercase from table Employee. 1

14. Is NULL value same as zero in SQL? If not, then what is the difference. 1

15. What is worm? 1

16. Name any two conditional statements in Python. 1

17. Give the output of the following code: 1

```
Str1="Python"
print(Str1[::-1])
```

18. What is the difference between char() and varchar() in SQL? 1

19. Differentiate between ftp and http. 1

20. Write SQL statement to display the structure of the table named Student; 1

21. What is Spam Mail? 1

SECTION – II

Consists of case study questions and are compulsory to attempt. Attempt any 4 sub parts from each question. Each sub part carries 1 mark. (4 + 4 = 8 marks)

22. Vishal is a database manager. He has been approached by a university to maintain the inventory of the students fees having the following details using SQL:

    - Name of the database – University
    - Name of the table – Fees
    - The attributes / fields of Fees relation are:

      AdmissionNo – character of size 3 (contains unique values)

      Course – character of size 25 (Not Null constraint)

      Fees – numeric value of type integer (default value as 50)

AdmissionNo	Course	SubjectSp	Fees
100001	BSc (H)	Biology	50000
100002	BSs (H)	Biology Chemistry	20000
100003	BSc (H)	Psychology	45000
100004	BA	NULL	10500
100005	BA (H)	Philosophy	20500

(a) Identify the primary key and mention the reason for choosing primary key. 1

(b) Write a DDL statement to create a database University and then write a statement to make use of this database. 1

(c) Write a DDL statement to create the table Fees with appropriate constraint. 1

(d) Write a DML statement to insert a record with some valid values. 1

(e) Write a DML statement to count the number of records having values in the SubjectSp field. 1

23. Anurag is writing a Python program for creating a csv file "Doctors.csv" to store the details of DNo, Name and Specialisation. He has written the following code and getting some of the errors and not able to fill in the blanks. Help him to solve his problem.

```
import csv

def Add_Docs(L1):
    a=open(_______________,'a',newline='')  #Line 1
    c=csv.writer(a)
    c.writerow(L1)
    a.close()

def Search_Sp(s):
    b=open("Doctor.csv",'r')
    cw=csv.reader(b)
    ________________             #Line 2
    for x in cw:
        if x[2]___s:             #Line 3
            print(x)
                                 #Line 4
            _________
    print("Total number of ",s," doctors: ",ctr)
    b.close()

P1=[1,"Aditi","Cardiology"]
P2=[2,"Priyanshu","Neurology"]
P3=[3,"Aditya","Cardiology"]
Add_Docs(P1)
Add_Docs(P2)
Add_Docs(P3)
Search_Sp("Cardiology")
```

(a) Fill in the blank for Line 1. 1

(b) Fill in the blank for Line 2 to initialise the counter variable used in the program. 1

(c) Fill in the blank for Line 3 for comparing the two values so as to display the records of doctors from cardiology department. 1

(d) Fill in the blank for Line 4 to increment the counter variable to keep track of number of doctors from cardiology department. 1

(e) Write the output of the program when executed. 1

PART – B

SECTION – I

Each question carries 2 marks **(2 × 10 = 20)**

24. Evaluate the following expressions: 2

(a) not (5>3 and 5<10) (b) 5 != 3

25. Define Hacker. 2

26. Write the full form of the following: 2

(a) ASP (b) JSP (c) PHP (d) WWW

27. What do you understand by local and global scope of variables? How can a global variable be accessed inside the function, if function has a variable with the same name? 2

28. Rewrite the following code in Python after removing all syntax error(s). Underline each correction done in the code. 2

```
for City in [Mumbai, Delhi, Calcutta, Madras]
    IF City[-1]==i:
        print(City)
```

29. What possible output(s) are expected to be displayed on screen at the time of execution of the program from the following code? Also, specify the minimum and maximum values that can be assigned to the variable N. 2

```
import random

N=random.randint(1,3)+2
TEXT="ABCDEFGHIJ"
for I in range(N):
    for J in range(N, 8):
        print(TEXT[J],end="")
    print()
```

(a) EFGH	(b) DEFGH	(c) ABC	(d) BCDE
EFGH	DEFGH	ABC	BCDE
EFGH	DEFGH	ABC	BCDE
EFGH			BCDE

30. Write the output of the following SQL queries: 2

(a) SELECT LEFT('CBSE EXAMINATION', 4);

(b) SELECT YEAR('2020-11-09');

31. Jaya has created a table TEACHER in the SCHOOL database with the following data: 2

ID	NAME	DEPARTMENT
1	ABHIMANYU	MATHS
2	AYAAN	SCIENCE
3	LAKSHAY	ENGLISH

Ayaan has left the job. She has written the Python code to delete the record of Ayaan from the table and getting few errors in the code and left those places as blank. Help her to fill up the blanks to execute the code successfully.

```
import mysql.connector
mydb=mysql.connector.connect(host="localhost",user="root",
                              passwd="root",database="SCHOOL")
mycursor=mydb.cursor()
s="________________________________________"        #Line 1
mycursor.execute(s)
mydb.______________             #Line 2
print("Deleted successfully")
mycursor.__________("SELECT * FROM TEACHER")     #Line 3
res=mycursor.fetchall()
for x in res:
    print(x)
```

(a) Write the SQL statement to fill in the blank for Line 1 to delete the record having name as Ayaan.

(b) Fill in the blank in Line 2 with a method which is used to save the changes made in the table.

(c) Fill in the blank in Line 3 with a method which is used to run the SQL statement which is passed as an argument to it.

(d) Write the output of the code when executed.

32. Write the use of RDBMS Selection operation with the help of an example. 2

33. What output will be generated when the following Python code is executed? 2

```
def calc():
    a=10
    while a>1:
        if(a%3==0):
            b=a%3
            a=a-1
        else:
            a=a-2
            b=a
        print(a**2)

calc()
```

SECTION – II

Each question carries 3 marks **(3 × 4 = 12)**

34. Write a user defined function ReArrange(L, N) in Python which should swap the contents of the first half locations of the List L with the contents of the second half locations. N is the size of the list. 3

For example, if list contains

L = [12, 3, 5, 7, 10, 4]

Then the function should rearrange the list and becomes:

L = [7, 10, 4, 12, 3, 5]

35. Assuming a text file named "country.txt" contains names of some countries written into it, write a function that reads the file "country.txt" and creates a new file named "new.txt" to contain names of only those countries which starts with a vowel (i.e. a, e, i, o, u) 3

For example, the contents of country.txt are:

Algeria Bangladesh Canada Brazil Angola Cuba Argentina France Australia Greece India Italy Russia Oman

Then the program will write the following into "new.txt":

Algeria Angola Argentina Australia India Italy Oman

36. Write the output for the following SQL queries (a) to (c) based on the relations TRAIN and PASSENGER given below: 3

Table: TRAIN			
TNO	**TNAME**	**ARRIVAL**	**DESTINATION**
12426	RAJDHANI	NEW DELHI	JAMMU
12425	RAJDHANI	JAMMU	NEW DELHI
12013	RAJDHANI	NEW DELHI	AMRITSAR
12014	RAJDHANI	AMRITSAR	NEW DELHI
12030	SWARNA SHATABDI	AMRITSAR	NEW DELHI

Table: PASSENGER					
PNR	**TNO**	**PNAME**	**GENDER**	**AGE**	**TRAVELDATE**
1	12426	A CHADHA	MALE	22	2020-09-21
2	12013	D NAYYAR	FEMALE	19	2020-09-21
3	12014	A K ARORA	FEMALE	23	2020-10-20
4	12425	P K SAXENA	MALE	NULL	2020-10-22

(a) SELECT COUNT(ARRIVAL), ARRIVAL FROM TRAIN GROUP BY ARRIVAL;

(b) SELECT COUNT(AGE) FROM PASSENGER;

(c) SELECT TNAME, PNAME FROM PASSENGER P, TRAIN T

WHERE P.TNO=T.TNO;

37. Write a function in python, MakePush(Package) and MakePop(Package) to add a new Package and delete a Package from a List of Package (PID, Description), considering them to act as push and pop operations of the Stack data structure. 3

SECTION – III

Each question carries 5 marks **(5 × 3 = 15)**

38. ABC Institute is starting up the network between its different wings. There are five buildings named ADMIN, JUNIOR, MIDDLE, SENIOR and HOSTEL. 5

You as a network expert have to suggest the best network related solutions for their problems raised in (a) to (e), keeping in mind the distances between the buildings and other given parameters.

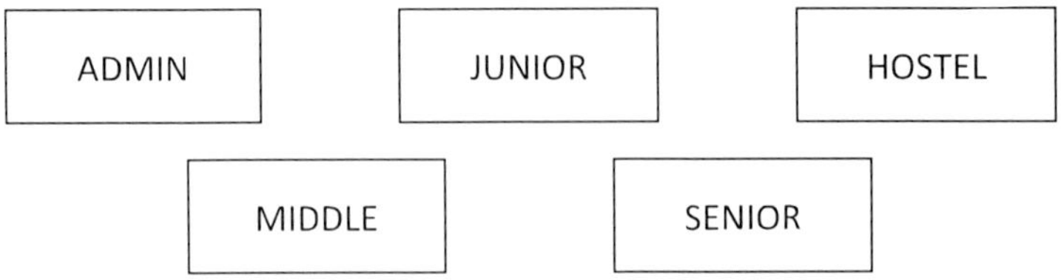

Distance between various buildings:

ADMIN TO JUNIOR	50 m
JUNIOR TO MIDDLE	75 m
MIDDLE TO ADMIN	65 m
SENIOR TO ADMIN	70 m
ADMIN TO HOSTEL	130 m

Number of computers installed at various buildings are:

ADMIN	100
JUNIOR	70
MIDDLE	80
SENIOR	90
HOSTEL	30

(a) Suggest the most suitable place to house the server with justification.

(b) Draw the cable layout to join the buildings and name the topology.

(c) Which hardware device is required to connect the computers within the same building?

(d) Suggest the placement of repeater (if any).

(e) Which one of the following will you suggest to establish the online face-to-face communication between the people of Admin Office to Hostel.

39. Write SQL commands for the following queries (a) to (e) based on the relations TRAIN and PASSENGER given in question number 36. 5

(a) To display details of all trains having the destination station New Delhi.

(b) To display the PNR, PNAME, GENDER, AGE of all passengers whose age is greater than 20 in descending order of their names.

(c) To display the details of passengers who are starting their journey from NEW DELHI.

(d) To display the total number of male and female passengers.

(e) To display the details of all the passengers travelling in the month of October.

40. The following employee data is stored in the form of binary file. 5

ENO	ENAME	DEPARTMENT
1	RIYA	ACCOUNTS
2	PRIYA	SALES
3	SHWETA	SALES

Now, Tanya wants to write the user defined functions in Python to perform the following tasks:

(a) To display all the records from the binary file "employee.dat".

(b) To modify name and department of a specified employee by searching that employee using ENO.

Self-Assessment Paper – 5 (Theory)

M.M.: 70 **Time: 3 hrs**

General Instructions

1. This question paper contains two parts A and B. Each part is compulsory.
2. Both Part A and Part B have choices.
3. Part-A has 2 sections:
    a. Section – I is short answer questions, to be answered in one word or one line.
    b. Section – II has two case studies questions. Each case study has 4 case-based subparts. An examinee is to attempt any 4 out of the 5 subparts.
4. Part - B is Descriptive Paper.
5. Part- B has three sections
    a. Section-I is short answer questions of 2 marks each in which two question have internal options.
    b. Section-II is long answer questions of 3 marks each in which two questions have internal options.
    c. Section-III is very long answer questions of 5 marks each in which one question has internal option.
6. All programming questions are to be answered using Python Language only.

PART – A

SECTION – I

Attempt any 15 questions from question numbers 1 to 21. Each question carries 1 mark. **(1 × 15 = 15 marks)**

1. Name the four types of tokens in Python. 1

2. Write the output of the following code segment: 1

```
Languages = ["Hindi", "English", "Bengali", "Punjabi", "French"]
Language = Languages[-1 : -6: -1]
print(Language)
```

3. Which of the following statements are true regarding the opening modes of a file? 1

(a) When a file is opened in read mode, it will give an error if the file doesn't exist.

(b) When a file is opened in write mode, it will give an error if the file doesn't exist.

(c) When a file is opened in write mode, it will overwrite the contents with new contents if the file exists.

(d) When a file is opened in read mode, it creates a new file if the file does not exist.

4. Write the name of the built-in function/ method to perform the following task: 1

(a) Returns a list after splitting the string at the specified separator.

(b) Converts the first character of each word to upper case.

5. Write any two assignment operators in Python. 1

6. Is a string mutable in Python? 1

7. When to use break statement in Python? 1

8. Name the Python Library modules which need to be imported to invoke the following functions: 1

(a) writeheader() (b) pow()

9. Name the internet communication protocol that protects the integrity and confidentiality of data between the user's computer and the site. 1

10. Define phishing. 1

11. Name any two aggregate functions (multiple row functions). 1

12. What is the use of check constraint in SQL? 1

13. Write SQL function to extract year from the date. 1

14. What will you do to search for a value in a table in SQL when you don't have the exact value to search for? 1

15. Name any two server-side scripting languages. 1

16. Name any two looping statements in Python. 1

17. Give the output of the following code: 1

```
Str1="Languages"
print(Str1[-1:-5:-1]
```

18. Which function in SQL is used to fetch the total number of records in a table? 1

19. Define virus. 1

20. Write SQL statement to display all the tables in the current database. 1

21. Give two examples of PAN and LAN type of networks. 1

SECTION – II

Consists of case study questions and are compulsory to attempt. Attempt any 4 sub parts from each question. Each sub part carries 1 mark. (4 + 4 = 8 marks)

22. Anurag is a database manager. He has been approached by a university to maintain the inventory of the candidates applying for admission in college having the following details using SQL:

- Name of the database – School
- Name of the table – Candidate
- The attributes / fields of Candidate relation are:

  RollNo – character of size 3 (contains unique values)

  Name – character of size 25 (Not Null constraint)

  Course – character of size 25

RollNo	Name	Course
100001	Srishti	Law
100002	Vaagish	Law
100003	Amit	Medical
100004	Rohan	NULL
100005	Rahul	Medical

(a) Identify the primary key and mention the reason for choosing primary key. 1

(b) Write a DDL statement to create a database School and then write a statement to make use of this database. 1

(c) Write a DDL statement to create the table Candidate with appropriate constraint. 1

(d) Write a DML statement to insert a record with some valid values. 1

(e) Write a DML statement to count the number of candidates applying for Law Course. 1

23. Anurag is writing a Python program for creating a csv file "Candidate.csv" to store the details of No, Name and Course. He has written the following code and getting some of the errors and not able to fill in the blanks. Help him to solve his problem.

```
import csv

def ADD(L1):
    a=open("Candidate.csv",'a',newline='')
    c=csv.writer(a)
    c.writerow(L1)
    a.close()
```

```
def Search(s):
    b=open("Candidate.csv",'r')
    cw=csv.reader(b)
    ctr=0
    for x in cw:
        if x[2]==s:
            print(x)
            ctr+=1
    print("Total number of ",s," candidates: ",ctr)
    b.close()

P1=[1,"Aditi","Medical"]
P2=[2,"Herman","Medical"]
P3=[3,"Preeti","Law"]
ADD(P1)
ADD(P2)
ADD(P3)
Search("Medical")
```

(a) Fill in the blank for Line 1. 1

(b) Fill in the blank for Line 2 to initialise the counter variable used in the program. 1

(c) Fill in the blank for Line 3 for comparing the two values so as to display the records of doctors from cardiology department. 1

(d) Fill in the blank for Line 4 to increment the counter variable to keep track of number of doctors from cardiology department. 1

(e) Write the output of the program when executed. 1

PART - B

SECTION – I

Each question carries 2 marks **(2 × 10 = 20)**

24. Evaluate the following expressions: 2

(a) 3*1**3 (b) False and True

25. Differentiate between virus and worm. 2

26. Write the full form of the following: 2

(a) TDMA (b) URL (c) IMAP (d) OSS

27. Ravi was asked to accept a list of even numbers but he did not put the relevant condition while accepting the list of numbers. Now you are required to write a code to convert all the odd numbers into even numbers by multiplying odd numbers by 2. 2

28. Rewrite the following code in Python after removing all syntax error(s). Underline each correction done in the code. 2

```
A "EXAMINATION"
for T in range[0, len(A)]:
    print(A(T))
print(T + A)
```

29. What possible output(s) are not expected to be displayed on screen at the time of execution of the program from the following code? Also specify the minimum and maximum values that can be assigned to the variable N. 2

```
import random
city_dir=['south','west','east','north']
N=random.randint(1,3)
new=""
for I in range(N, 0, -1):
    new=new+city_dir[I]
print(new)
```

(i) northeastwest

(ii) east

(iii) eastwest

(iv) northeastwestsouth

30. Write the output of the following SQL queries: 2

(a) SELECT MID('CBSE EXAMINATION', 6, 4);

(b) SELECT MONTHNAME('2020-11-09');

31. Sanchita has the created a table MEMBER in the LIBRARY database with the following data: 2

ID	NAME
1	Diya
2	Mauli
3	Aastha

She has written the Python code to insert a new record with the following data (4, 'Shreya'). But she is getting few errors in the code and left those places as blank. Help her to fill up the blanks to execute the code successfully.

```
import mysql.connector
mydb=mysql.connector.connect(host="localhost",user="root",
                              passwd="root",database="LIBRARY")
mycursor=mydb.cursor()
s="INSERT_______________ VALUES(4,'SHREYA')"  #Line 1
mycursor._______________      #Line 2
mydb.commit()
print("Row added successfully")
mycursor.execute("SELECT * FROM MEMBER")
res=mycursor.fetchall()
for x in ____:            #Line 3
    print(x)
```

(a) Complete the SQL statement to insert the record in Line 1.

(b) Fill in the blank for Line 2 to run the SQL statement written in line 1.

(c) Fill in the blank in Line 3 to iterate over the list to get all the records one by one.

(d) Write the output of the code.

32. Write SQL query to create a table 'Player' with the following structure: 2

Attribute/ Field	Type	Constraint
PID	Integer	Primary Key
PName	Varchar(20)	NOT NULL
Sport	Varchar(15)	DEFAULT='CRICKET'
DOB	Date	

33. What output will be generated when the following Python code is executed? 2

```
def output(STR):
    Count=3
    for I in range(len(STR)):
        S=STR[Count]
        SUM=float(S) + I
        print(SUM)
        Count-=1

STR=["90","20","50","40"]
output(STR)
```

SECTION – II

Each question carries 3 marks **(3 × 4 = 12)**

34. Write a user defined function AddOddEven(List1) to display sum of odd and even values separately from the list of values in List1. 3

For example: If the List contain

List1 = [15, 26, 37, 10, 22, 13]

The function should display:

Sum of even values: 58

Sum of odd values: 65

35. Write a user define function countvow() in Python to count and display the number of vowels in a text file named "Article.txt". 3

36. Consider the table STUDENT given below and write the output for the following SQL queries (a) to (c) based on the relation STUDENT: 3

SNO	NAME	CLASS	DOB	GENDER	MARKS
1	SANJAY	XI	06/03/2002	M	450
2	RUDRA	XII	12/04/2003	M	465
3	ADITYA	XI	12/10/2002	M	365
4	AYUSH	XI	20/09/2002	M	380
5	KIRTI	XII	24/10/2003	F	395

(a) SELECT NAME FROM STUDENT WHERE CLASS='XI' AND NAME LIKE 'A%'

(b) SELECT CLASS, AVG(MARKS) FROM STUDENT
GROUP BY CLASS;

(c) SELECT GENDER, COUNT(*) FROM STUDENT
GROUP BY GENDER;

37. Write Addnew(Employee) and Remove(Employee) methods in Python to add a new employee and remove an employee from a list of employees, considering them to act as a PUSH and POP operations of the data structure Stack. 3

SECTION – III

Each question carries 5 marks **(5 × 3 = 15)**

38. The Mango Pvt. Ltd has set up its new centre at Hyderabad for its office and web based activities, it has four blocks of buildings as shown in the diagram. 5

You as a network expert have to suggest the best network related solutions for their problems raised in (a) to (e), keeping in mind the distances between the buildings and other given parameters.

Distance between various buildings:

Block A to Block B	50 m
Block B to Block C	145 m
Block C to Block D	65 m
Block A to Block D	80 m
Block B to Block D	40 m
Block A to Block C	110 m

Number of computers installed at various buildings are:

Block A	40
Block B	52
Block C	150
Block D	1

(a) Suggest the most suitable place to house the server with justification.

(b) Suggest suitable cable layout(s) for joining the blocks.

(c) Which hardware device is required to connect the computers within the same building?

(d) Suggest the placement of repeater (if any).

(e) Which of the following communication media, will you suggest to be procured by the company for connecting to a new branch office in New Delhi for very effective and fast communication?

- Ethernet cable
- Optical Fiber
- Telephone cable

39. Write SQL commands for the following queries (a) to (e) based on the relation SALESMAN with the following data: 5

ID	NAME	SALARY	BONUS (%)	DOJ
A01	NISHA SURI	7000	5	29-10-2019
A02	GAUTAM	8000	7	13-03-2018
A03	TINA SARKAR	6700	NULL	18-03-2017
A04	MEENU CHUGH	4500	4	23-01-2018
A05	MEETA SHARMA	8700	NULL	22-12-2018
A06	TRIPTI	4500	8	18-03-2019

(a) Display salesman name and bonus amount from tables Salesman. Bonus amount is to be calculated as bonus percentage on Salary.

(b) Display the number of salesman having salary greater than 6500.

(c) Display the details of salesman whose name is having 'a' anywhere.

(d) Display name and salary of those salesman from the table salesman where the length of the name is exactly 6 characters.

(e) Display the details of all those salesman who joined in the year 2018.

40. The following player data is stored in the form of binary file Player.dat: 5

ID	NAME	SPORT
1	DEVANSH	FOOTBALL
2	ABHIMANYU	JIU JUTSU
3	NOBOJIT	JIU JUTSU
4	SWASTIK	FOOTBALL
5	ARYAN	FOOTBALL
6	DIVYANSH	JIU JUTSU

Srishti wants to write code in Python to perform the following tasks:

(a) User defined function Display() to display all the records from the binary file "Player.dat".

(b) User defined function DelePlayer(N) to delete the player from the binary file "Player.dat" whose name N is passed as an argument to this function.